THE LITTLE COR

SOUP SALAD & STUFF COOKBOOK

Beatriz Treloar

WillowOrchard Publishing

A view from the Treloar family farm near Zennor

Introduction

I grew up on a farm in north west Cornwall. Cove Farm has been in the Treloar family for generations, originally mixed arable with Dexter cattle, pictured above a Cornish beach on the first page, and westcountry longwool sheep. But when my father Jago and his mates boarded a Brittany Ferries sailing after a rugby club do, thinking he was bound for Roscoff, he ended up in Santander! Here he met Inés di Santangel, a vegetarian from an arable farm in Castile Leon, and the rest is my history!

Mamá grew up with legumes: chickpeas, lentils and beans and my parents made Cove Farm into a successful fruit and vegetable grower. Whilst I was raised vegetarian and pescatarian my partner's family, the Nancarrows, has introduced me to the joys of quality sustainable meat and poultry.

So while my first book featured fish and seafood, my second expands the larder to include meat and poultry, plus some more fish and seafood and of course, vegetables. This book brings you soups, salads and stuff. And what is stuff you ask? Well, think of a full-flavoured bowlful you can eat with a spoon, on a sofa, on a beach, on a picnic or of course, at a table. And I had to include some more easy, reliable gluten-free baking staples.

I always source my meat - like my fish and seafood – locally, meat from small abattoirs, through independent butchers and farm shops. You will find great quality and reasonable prices especially if you get to know your suppliers. I understand that supermarkets are convenient and they can offer quality and value, but if you are able to support your local independents as well, I do urge you to do so.

We were brought up to be thrifty. Mamá instilled in us respect for ingredients; making the most of them and wasting nothing. A perfect example of this ethos is in my Green Soup, a flexible and healthy delight!

My camping friendly, one or no-pan recipes, are identified by my ▲ icon!

As in my first book, The Little Cornish Fish & Seafood Cookbook, all the recipes are dairy and gluten-free, but you can substitute dairy and gluten products in equal measures.

3

Gluten-free baking gets a bad press. People think it is difficult and unforgiving but trust me this is just not true. I make no apologies for including my gluten-free baking staples again; you will find them used in new recipes. As in all baking, the investment in a good quality flour will be rewarded by the results.

I hope you will enjoy some more flavours from my Cornish life and will take pleasure in bringing some new creations to your repertoire.

Crab shells, including the spider crab's, make a great stock (see the Soup section). Amazingly tasty, very useful, very thrifty!

Saludos and best wishes.......Beatriz Treloar

With thanks and love to my family and friends for their suggestions and tasting expertise and as ever, to my dear friend, Ochre Pengelly, for her drawings.

Ingredients notes and measures

For those who do not eat "free from", dairy can be substituted for the goats', sheeps' and plant-based ingredients used here. Plant-based includes oat, soya, coconut, almond and other nuts.

So, where oat milk or oat cream is used, you can substitute dairy milk or double cream, and dairy yoghurt where I've used goat's or sheep's.

For those with no gluten issues any pastry, bread flours and bread can be used. Just go for quality.

For the pasties, Jus Rol make a gluten-free pastry variety, but the crispy butter pastry here is really easy to make.

Where I use soy sauce my recipes call for Tamari soy sauce which has no gluten, but feel free to use any soy sauce if there are no gluten issues.

Where I use groundnut oil, again any flavourless oil such as vegetable, sunflower or rapeseed will work.

Good olive oil = extra virgin olive oil

A glug = 25 ml

A slug = 40 ml

A splash = 10 ml

...........approximately!

An egg is a large free range egg.

All measurements are metric.

To blitz (soup) is to whizz, to blend, with a stick blender. Or a liquidizer or food processor if you like smooth rather than chunky soup.

With all the gluten-free baking recipes I use a rubber spatula or a metal palette knife to mix the wet ingredients into the dry, NEVER my hands!

SOUP

Stock

Good stock is really easy to make and well worth the effort because it makes soups even more flavoursome than they would be without this great foundation. It's also a great way of getting the most out of the food you buy and grow because you're using things you might otherwise throw away or put onto the compost heap.

Stock makes a great base for soups, and reduced it makes incredibly tasty sauces and gravies. My approach is to keep most of the basic ingredients the same for most flavours of stock: poultry, fish, shellfish, green and vegetable. Asparagus stock is a little different. It's a fantastic base for asparagus breakfast soup and covered in the recipe on page 23.

Basics:

carrots, 2, or 1 large, washed and roughly chopped (or beetroot for my pink stew on page 97)

bay leaves, 9, scrunched up in your hand to release flavours

black peppercorns, 11

large onion, 1 peeled and roughly chopped

celery, 2 sticks, tops off, bottom rooty bits trimmed off, roughly chopped

leek, 1, top and any bottom rooty bits trimmed off, cleaned, roughly chopped

time; 2 hours for poultry, green and vegetable; 1½ hours for shellfish; 45 minutes for fish. If using fish heads, remove after the first 7 poaching minutes, flake off the flesh and return the heads if you want the flesh for fishcakes!

You'll also need a 7 litre stockpot or a large saucepan or medium Le Creuset if making a smaller amount.

All my stocks freeze well.

Chicken and other birds

Whatever the bird, poultry makes a great stock, for soups, sauces and gravies, or to be used as a flavoursome liquor in curries and stews. It doesn't have to be cooked, so while most of us will be making stock from a roasted bird carcass, an uncooked carcass is absolutely fine and the results will be just as good if not better!

The instructions are the same whether you're using a cooked carcass, skin and bones or raw.

A roast chicken stock beginning to bubble up with a lovely aroma

Just make sure you keep all the bones and left over skin from the poultry meals you serve up as well as the carcass, keeping them in a bag in the freezer until you're ready to make the stock if you're not stocking up straight away.

Chicken, turkey, goose, duck, pheasant, and guinea fowl all contribute their delicious individual flavours to the stock, and are the stars of the finished soup, sauce or gravy.

13

Break up the carcass so that it takes up less space, two or three pieces will be fine. If you're using a whole turkey or goose carcass, which are larger than most chickens, simply increase the basic ingredients accordingly. If you're using smaller birds such as pheasant or partridge use more than one carcass if you have them or reduce the other ingredients accordingly.

Then put the carcass, bones and skin that you have saved into the stockpot, followed by the basics (page 12; carrots, or beetroot for pink stew on page 97, bay leaves, black peppercorns, onion, celery, leek), then top up with water to 25mm – 50mm below top of stockpot.

Bring to the boil, turn the heat down and simmer for two hours. Use the lid to manage the rate of liquor evaporation, leaving it off if it is going too slowly, putting it on and leaving a gap if it is going too quickly.

Strain the liquor and bones/skin/vegetables into a large bowl or two, through a colander, pressing down (using a hand is easiest, once it's cool enough) on the mush to extract ALL the juice.

As it is cooking the stock will give off a wonderful aroma and I can tell you that the cats at Mamá's and Félipe's love it, hanging around the kitchen and staring up at the cooker top whenever I make chicken stock there! They always appreciate it when I pick through the strained liquor and vegetable mush at the end, putting the by now well-cooked poultry pieces onto a saucer for them.

Chicken and other bird stock freezes extremely well, so if you have no immediate plans for it simply ladle it into two or three freezer bags, making sure they're completely cold before putting them into the freezer.

Fish stock

The bones and heads (frames as they're often called by fishmongers), as well as skin, of most fish can be used to make fish stock, but I steer clear of using mackerel or other oily fish such as salmon, trout or sardines.

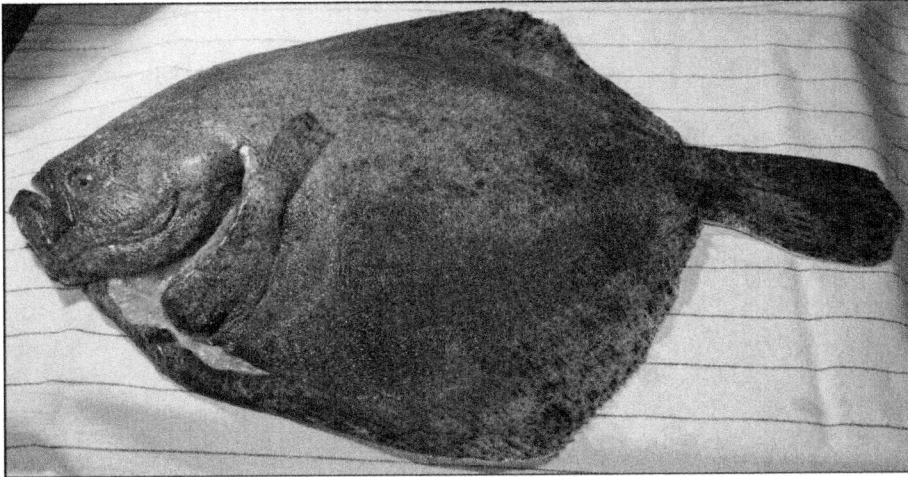

**A beautiful turbot, great poached whole or for filleting.
If your fishmonger fillets it, ask for the frame!**

If you're used to buying just fillets of fish from a fishmonger, ask if he or she will let you have a couple of frames including the heads as you're going to make some stock. They'll usually pick them out of their frames bin and bag them up at no cost!! If it's a frame from your own fillets, chosen from a fish you've selected you'll already have paid for them anyway as the weight will have been included in the total weight of fish you're charged for.

If you're lucky enough to get a large head or two, of a cod or haddock say, this will give you enough meat to make a good few fish cakes, in which case follow the 7 minute poaching suggestion below.

While the flesh of fish certainly makes great stock, what I love is making use of the whole fish, so in the restaurant as well as at home we always use frames only for the stock, serving the fillets and steaks mostly as starters and mains.

Cod, haddock, pollack, gurnard, ray, john dory, lemon sole, the backbone and skin of monkfish, turbot . . the list could go on! Only use raw fish frames though, not cooked

If you've been hoarding a growing number of frames in the freezer until you've got enough for a good batch of stock, use the stockpot. You'll always get more in the pot than you think, as the frames break up as they cook.

Simply put the fishy pieces, broken up if they're too long and skin that you have saved into the stockpot, followed by the basics (page 12; carrots, bay leaves, black peppercorns, onion, celery, leek), then top up with water to 25mm - 50mm below top of stockpot.

Bring to the boil, turn the heat down and simmer for 45 minutes. Use the lid to manage the rate of liquor evaporation, leaving it off if it is going too slowly, putting it on and leaving a gap if it is going too quickly.

Strain the liquor and bones/skin/vegetables into a large bowl or two, through a colander, pressing down (using a hand is easiest, once it's cool enough) on the mush to extract ALL the juice.

If you're lucky enough to have picked up large fish heads from the fishmonger, try just poaching them in the stock mix for 7 minutes once it has been brought to a simmer. Remove them carefully using a large slotted spoon and set them on a plate, then flake off the meat with a fork. Set the meat aside for making fishcakes later and put what's left back into the stock. You might be surprised how much meat there is!

Fish stock freezes extremely well, so if you have no immediate plans for it simply ladle it into two or three freezer bags and put it in the freezer, making sure it is completely cold before putting the bags into the freezer.

Fish stock can be reduced and made into great sauces, used as a base for soups, for creating a pan-made sauce as you're frying fish, hake or huss for example, mixed with chicken stock as a paella liquor, or wherever else you think you can use it. It's one of those things that's great to have in the freezer as you never know when you might need it or what for.

Seafood stock

The shells of cooked crabs, lobsters and prawns, as well as the shells of uncooked prawns can be used to make this, my favourite, stock.

If your fishmonger sells crabmeat, claws, or whole cooked crab he or she will probably be able to supply you with crab shells if you're not buying any shell-on crab. If you're buying lobster just save the shells in the freezer, they freeze well, as do all seafood shells., until you make the stock. The shells of large prawns can be removed from uncooked prawns before you cook them, try them with monkfish in a spiced tomato and coriander sauce (page 83), and add great flavour to a seafood stock.

Two crab or large lobster shells, with whatever prawn shells you've got saved up, will be enough for a flavoursome stock.

A wonderful cooked spider crab ready for the meat to be picked. The shell gives amazing sweet flavour to a seafood stock.

-Simply put the shells, (upside down for the body shells to save space) that you have saved into the stockpot, followed by the basics (page 12; carrots, bay leaves, black peppercorns, onion, celery, leek), then top up with water to 25mm - 50mm below top of stockpot.

Bring to the boil, turn the heat down and simmer for 1½ hours. Use the lid to manage the rate of liquor evaporation, leaving it off if it is going too slowly, putting it on and leaving a gap if it is going too quickly.

Lift out as many of the larger pieces of shell as you can with a slotted spoon then strain the liquor and shells/vegetables into a large bowl or two, through a colander. Press (using a hand carefully to avoid sharp shell edges is easiest, once it's cool) on the mush to extract ALL the juice.

Seafood stock freezes extremely well, so if you have no immediate plans for it simply ladle it into two or three freezer bags and put it in the freezer, making sure it is completely cold before putting the bags into the freezer.

Seafood stock can be reduced and made into amazing sauces and gravies to accompany plainly poached, pan fried or baked fish, used as a base for soups, like fish stock it too can be mixed with chicken stock to make a paella liquor. It's also a fabulous liquor to use in fish and / or seafood curries. It's another 'great to have' in the freezer at home.

Green stock

I call this green stock because it's, well . . . green! I first made it a long time ago when I was helping Mamá clear space for new plantings in the greenhouse and vegetable garden and I realised that what we were pulling and digging up would be going straight onto the compost heaps. Why do that I thought, when we could be using it to make stocks and soups! It's great, among other things as a base for rocket and dill, and courgette and tomato soups. And of course not forgetting green soup!

Nasturtium leaves make a great addition to green stock, especially if you don't have much rocket, and the flowers a lovely garnish on green soup

Wild rocket, New Zealand spinach and nasturtiums always grow strongly and spread widely in the greenhouses, and there is always plenty of dill, fennel and coriander too. These all spread as they grow, flower, seed, and self sow. So the paths get overgrown and we have to trim the plants back three or four times each year to make space for new plantings and to be able to walk between the beds to weed and harvest!

So, I used a couple of large trugs full of these old plants to make stock! The rocket, spinach and nasturtium leaves contribute most of the bright green colour as well as giving up their delicious flavours, especially the rocket, whose flavour was a real surprise when I first tried it. The woody stems of the dill, fennel, and coriander add amazing flavour too. Garlic and elephant garlic self- seed too so if they are picked to make way for new plants I also use their dry woody stems.

To make smaller quantities than I usually do you can buy the ingredients from your greengrocer.

First make sure the plants are shaken well to set loose any critters that may be hiding, then trim the roots off and rinse everything thoroughly.

To be able to comfortably fit as much as possible into a large stockpot chop the stems and leaves into 10cm, 4in, lengths and pop them in the stock pot. Then add the basics (page 12; carrots, bay leaves, black peppercorns, onion, celery, leek), mix them all up and top up with water until 25mm – 50mm below top of stockpot. Press the leaves and stems down below the water level if possible, don't worry too much though if some are awkward and refuse to go below the water as they will naturally reduce in volume as the stock cooks through.

Bring to the boil, then reduce the heat so that the stock is simmering nicely and leave it for a couple of hours, stirring every twenty minutes or so.

Then remove the stems and leaves using a slotted spoon, placing them into a large sieve or colander sitting over a large bowl and when cool enough squash them down to get as much juice from them as possible before tipping them into a large pan to take them NOW to the compost.

Finally, pour the stock through the sieve or colander into the bowl and when cool enough pour into two or three freezer bags if you're not going to use it all straight away. When completely cold take them to the freezer.

What a great way to intervene in the journey of these luscious flavours on their way to the garden compost!

Vegetable stock

For a more flavoursome vegetable stock simply use a higher proportion of the basics (page 12; carrots, bay leaves, black peppercorns, onion, celery, leek) to water than you would to make any of the other stocks.

Vegetable stock is an ideal base for meat curries, onion and other gravies, and vegetable soups including celeriac, roasted butternut squash, and courgette and tomato.

So, for a stockpot or large Le Creuset use 4 large carrots, chopped, 12 bay leaves scrunched, 20 black peppercorns, 2 large onions, peeled and chopped, 4 sticks of celery, chopped and 2 leeks, topped and tailed and sliced. For a large saucepan use half these quantities, and for a medium saucepan use a quarter.

If you have vegetables that are past their best for serving as part of a meal such as peppers, cauliflower, broccoli, turnip or courgettes, or anything else you fancy trying you can chop them and add them, too. It's just a personal thing, but I don't use swede, squash, pumpkin, or celeriac in vegetable stock but don't let that stop you trying them if you'd like to give them a go.

Simply put the chopped ingredients in the pan, add water until 25 - 50mm below the top, then bring to the boil over a high heat. Then reduce the heat and simmer the stock for an hour, two if you have the time.

Then strain the stock through a colander into a large bowl, pressing the vegetables firmly when cool enough using your hand is easiest , to make sure you collect as much of the lovely flavour as possible.

Like the other stocks, vegetable stock freezes really well, so if you're not going to use it straight away ladle it into two or three freezer bags and when completely cold put them in the freezer.

Artichoke - Jerusalem - soup, with asparagus

Jerusalem artichokes, 4, outer leaves removed, chopped

onions, medium, 1½, peeled and chopped

red chilli, 1, chopped, include seeds if you like it hot

asparagus, 8 spears, woody ends removed, chopped

groundnut oil, 1 glug

chicken stock, 1 litre

2 portions

Heat the soup pan over a medium heat and when hot add the oil, then all the ingredients apart from 3 asparagus spears and the stock. When the onions are soft and translucent add the stock and bring to the boil, then reduce to a simmer.

Simmer for 30 minutes then blitz with a stick blender, return to the heat and bring back to the simmer. Add the remaining asparagus and simmer for another 5 minutes

Remove from the heat, ladle into bowls and eat.............a tasty starter with one ladle, or light lunch with 2 ladles and a slice or two of bread.

Asparagus breakfast soup, with poached eggs and crispy pancetta

The pancetta is especially for my sister Lucia who adores this soup.

asparagus ends – from snapping the stalks when you've had asparagus, saved in the freezer - ideally 18 or more, sliced in half lengthways

shallots, 2, peeled and fine chopped (small onions are fine if you don't have shallots)

goats' butter, 2 knobs

vegetable oil, ½ glug

asparagus spears, medium or thick, 3 or 4 per person, woody ends removed as above, chopped into 12mm pieces

mushrooms, button, ideally chestnut, medium, 4, sliced

eggs, 4

white wine vinegar, 1 tablespoon

pancetta, 2 slices, fried until crispy, then broken into medium squares, (optional) If you don't want to use the pancetta try grating a little Parmesan or Pecorino cheese (ewes' milk cheese) over the soup at the end.

2 portions

This soup is wonderful for breakfast! Ideally make the stock the night before though; it takes an hour at least.

Put asparagus ends and 1 shallot into 1 litre of water, simmer at least 1 hour, ideally 2, top up occasionally with more water to stop drying out. Strain the stock into a bowl then squeeze the asparagus and shallot into the bowl to extract all their juices.

Heat medium pan over medium heat, add 1 knob of goats' butter, and when melted add the other shallot. Fry gently for 5 minutes then add HALF the asparagus. Fry for 10 minutes, add the stock to the pan, bring to the boil, simmer for 30 minutes. While this is happening, melt the last of the goats' butter in a small pan, and when hot add the mushrooms. Fry and turn for 10 minutes, remove, and dry on kitchen towel.

When the soup has had 30 minutes, blitz with a blender, add the rest of the asparagus and the mushrooms, and simmer for 6 minutes. Have a kettle of boiling water to hand.

Serve the soup into preheated bowls. Add recently boiled water to the soup pan, return to the boil, add the vinegar, carefully break the eggs into the water and poach gently FOR 1 MINUTE.

When whites are still translucent lift the eggs out carefully, and float onto the soup. Sprinkle with the pancetta, if using, and serve.

Fantastic way to use up all those asparagus ends. Stunning.

Blue cheese and broccoli soup ▲

broccoli, large head, broken into florets, plus stalk, chopped

potato, 1 medium, peeled and small cubed

onion, 1 medium, chopped

garlic, 1 clove, finely chopped

leek, 1 small, chopped

vegetable stock, 1 litre

blue cheese - Cornish blue, Stilton or blue goats', 100 gm

goats' butter, 1 knob

crème fraîche, 125gm or double or oat cream, 125gm plus 1 tspn lemon juice

flavourless oil, glug

1/8 tsp nutmeg

salt & pepper to taste

4 large portions

Bring the vegetable stock to the boil, add the broccoli and simmer for 5 minutes then remove the broccoli and set aside.

Melt the butter and oil in a large pan then sweat the onions, garlic, leek and potato for 10 minutes.

Add the reserved broccoli and stock and simmer for 20 minutes.

Add the blue cheese, crème fraîche or cream and lemon juice, nutmeg and black pepper and cook for a further 10 minutes. Taste and add salt accordingly.

This makes a wonderful winter lunch.

Variations: also works with a leafy spinach with stalks, or chard with stalks, in place of broccoli

Chicken soup - spicy, with lettuce

chicken stock, 1½ litres

onion, 1, medium, peeled and chopped

garlic, 3 cloves, peeled and crushed

red chillies, 2, chopped, with seeds if you like it hot

good olive oil 2 good glugs

ginger, fresh, 2 good thumbs, leave unpeeled if you like hotter and spicier, or peel if you prefer less hot and spicy, chopped into fine matchsticks

coriander, fresh, chopped with leaves, 1 very good handful

potato, medium 1, peeled chopped into small cubes for thickening

spring onions, 4, topped and tailed, thinly sliced

lettuce, little gem, 1, quartered

2 portions

Heat the soup pan over a medium heat and when hot add the oil, then the onion garlic and chillies. Fry, stirring occasionally, until the onions are soft and translucent.

Add the stock and potato, and bring to the boil then reduce to a simmer and continue until it is reduced by half, to concentrate the flavours. Now blitz with a blender to break up the onions.

Bring back to a simmer, add the ginger, five minutes later add the spring onions and remove from the heat.

Put one quarter of the lettuce in each of 2 soup bowls and ladle the soup over. Garnish with the coriander.

This is a simple soup but with great flavours and aromas while cooking-delicious either as a starter or a light lunch.

Chicken soup - with spring onions, coriander, and sweetcorn

chicken stock, 2 litres

spring onions, 6, topped and tailed, chopped

toasted sesame oil, 2 glugs

ginger, fresh, 2 thumbs, leave unpeeled for hotter and spicier or peel if you prefer, grated

coriander, fresh, good handful, including stalks, chopped

sweetcorn, 2 cobs

potato, medium, 1, peeled and chopped into small cubes, for thickening (it will dissolve)

4 portions

First, add the stock and potato to the pan and reduce the stock to ¾ litre by simmering without the lid for around 60 minutes until it is very "chickenny", adding the sesame oil and ginger after 15 minutes.

While the stock is simmering strip the corn kernels from the cobs by using a knife; hold the cobs upright on a board and stroke the knife downwards between the kernels and body of the cob.

Add the corn to the pan and simmer for another 5 minutes, then add the spring onions, simmer for a further 5 minutes. Serve into bowls, and with a final flourish, garnish with the coriander,

Chicken soup, balsamic style, with sweetcorn

chicken breasts, 2

chicken stock, 1½ litres

sweetcorn, fresh, 2

onion, 1, chopped, or shallots, 2 – 3, chopped

potato, medium, 1, peeled and chopped into small cubes to – to thicken

balsamic vinegar, 2 glugs

flavourless oil, 2 glugs

4 portions

Preheat the oven to 170º C, 150ºC fan. Use a skewer to pierce the chicken breasts several times on both sides then place them on a square of foil and sprinkle the balsamic vinegar over and massage it well before bringing the edges of the foil together to make a parcel. Put it on a baking tray or Pyrex dish just in case it leaks! The idea here is to infuse the balsamic flavour through the chicken. You don't want to fully cook the chicken at this stage, so put the tray in the oven for 20 minutes.

While the chicken is cooking, strip the sweetcorn kernels using a sharp knife drawn down the cob lengthways. Now, put the soup pan on a medium heat and when hot add the oil, onion or shallots, half the sweetcorn, and the potato, stirring every couple of minutes (if you don't the sweetcorn kernels and potato might stick). When the onion / shallots are soft and translucent (after around 5 minutes) add the stock and bring to a simmer.

Remove the chicken from the oven after 20 minutes and open the parcel carefully to avoid being scalded by the steam. Break up the chicken, shred it, and put half into the soup. Now reduce the soup by about half to really condense those flavours by simmering for 1 hour, stirring every 5 minutes.

Almost there now; blitz the soup with a stick blender, add the remaining chicken and sweetcorn, simmer for another 10 minutes; then serve.

Duck & cherry soup, Eastern style

duck stock, 1½ - 2 litres

onions, 2, skinned and chopped

cherries, black, 20 – 25, pitted, each chopped into 8 pieces

red chilli, ½ - 1, finely chopped, with seeds if you like it hot

toasted sesame oil, 3 good glugs

Chinese 5 spice, 1 tablespoon

dried ginger, 2 teaspoons

fresh coriander, chopped, 1 handful

spring onions, 3, topped and tailed, sliced

salt to taste

4 portions

Heat the oil in the soup pan, then add the onions, cherries and half the chilli and fry gently until the onions are soft and translucent (around 5 minutes). Add the stock, bring to the boil. Now add 1 tablespoon of the Chinese 5 spice and 1 teaspoon of the dried ginger; don't add all at once because you're going to test for taste after around 15 minutes.

Now, you're going to reduce the soup to intensify the flavours by simmering for 1 hour, testing for taste after 15 minutes. If you want more of a kick, or a more spicy flavour, add a little more chilli or ginger . . . or more of everything if you like.

Test again after another 15 minutes. When I was developing this recipe, I did 3 taste tests, and added more chilli every time. You don't want it so hot it burns and kills the lovely flavours – just enough to give a real chilli sensation, but leaving the other flavours intact.

When reduced to around one third of the original volume, blitz well with a blender and taste. Add salt to taste.

Get the soup bowls ready and ladle in, adding coriander and spring onions to garnish, then serve while piping hot.

What a great way to use the duck carcase!

Duck & orange noodle soup with bean sprouts and watercress

When making the stock for this soup add 1 thumb of grated fresh ginger, or add it at the onion stage below if you're using a made duck stock.

duck stock, ¾ litre reduced from 1½ - 2 litres

onion, medium, 1 peeled and chopped

toasted sesame oil, 2 glugs

orange, large, zest of ½ of the orange

orange, large, juice of ½ of the orange

noodles, around 100gm. Use ½ the quantity of dough made on page 143 and freeze the rest for later, or 100gm from a bought packet of egg noodles

bean sprouts, 1 handful

watercress, chopped, 1 handful

3 – 4 portions

Add the oil to pan and when hot, add the onion, lightly frying until translucent and soft, around 5 minutes). Then add the stock and bring to the boil, simmer without the lid, adding the orange zest when it begins to simmer. Taste for "orangeyness" after 15 minutes, add zest until you're happy with the taste (don't forget, you'll be adding the juice at the end).

Now, be careful, you don't want to overcook the noodles and bean sprouts; they only need 2 – 3 minutes so they go in right at the end (for bought noodles, check packet for cooking time and adjust accordingly). If you're not ready to serve, turn off the heat and then reheat the soup so it is back to a simmer just before you are ready.

Add the orange juice, noodles and bean sprouts when you're ready to serve, and leave simmering for just 2 – 3 minutes, then ladle into bowls and garnish with the chopped watercress.

Delicious and easy, with great flavour and textures.

Duck soup, with lettuce or stir-fried pak choi

duck stock, well reduced, 1½ litres

onions, medium, 2

rocket, good handful, chopped

toasted sesame oil, 2 good glugs

spring onions, 3, topped and tailed, sliced

lettuce, little gem, 1, ¼'d or pak choi, 2, ¼'d and stir-fried for 2 minutes in sesame oil just before soup is served

4 portions

Put the oil into a warmed soup pan, when it is warm add the onions, gently fry until soft and translucent, around 4 - 5 minutes, then add stock and rocket.

Simmer without lid until volume is reduced by around one third (allow up to 45 minutes), remove from heat and blitz. Add the spring onions.

To serve, place 2 quarters of lettuce or four quarters of stir-fried pak choi in each soup bowl then ladle the soup over.

Serve, then slurp and munch away at this flavourful soup dish with the unusual crunch.

Duck soup, with orange, and exotic mushrooms

duck stock, well reduced, 1½ litres

mushrooms, exotic (shitake and / or oyster), 10, sliced

coriander, fresh, chopped, 1 handful

orange, large, 1, zest of around ½ the orange, juice of ½ the orange

onion, 1, peeled and chopped

rocket, chopped, 1 handful

toasted sesame oil, 2 glugs

spring onions, 3, topped and tailed, sliced

red chilli, 1 chopped, seeds out unless you like it hot

4 portions

Put the oil into a warmed soup pan and heat, when warm add onion, chilli, and orange zest. Stir-fry until onions are translucent and soft (around 5 minutes) then add the stock, rocket, and half the mushrooms. Simmer with the lid off for 30 minutes.

Blitz, add the orange juice, bring back to the boil and simmer for another 30 minutes. The aroma should be delicious by now!

Add the rest of the mushrooms and the spring onions, simmer for another 5 minutes. All done!

Simply ladle into soup bowls and lastly garnish with the coriander.

Green soup

The main flavour for my green soup is the ingredient that happens to be the most plentiful or inexpensive at the time, this recipe having originated from plants that would have normally found their way to the compost heap when we were clearing space in Mamá's greenhouses for new plantings a few years ago. Here, the focus is on spinach, but it could equally be on rocket.

spinach, 8 good handfuls, including the more tender stalks, roughly chopped

dill, fronds with the more tender stalks, roughly chopped, 4 handfuls

fennel, tender stalks and bulbous joints, chopped, 2 handfuls

coriander including stalks, chopped, 1 handful

onions, 1, peeled, finely chopped

potatoes, medium, 4, peeled and chopped. 2 into small cubes, ½cm, 2 into medium cubes , 1½cm

garlic, peeled, 3 cloves, crushed

vegetable oil, 4 tbspn

green stock, 3 litres

salt, ground black pepper, white pepper (we like lots), to taste

Portions. This will make around 12 – 16 portions depending on how deep your soup bowls are! Green soup freezes really well so bag up what you don't use and freeze for later.

Put a large soup pan with the vegetable oil over a medium heat, when warm add the chopped onion and garlic and fry gently until the onions are soft and translucent, about 5 - 7 minutes.

Add the potatoes and fry for another 5 minutes, stirring frequently to stop the potatoes sticking.

Add the leaves and stock and stir well, turn up the heat to bring to the boil then reduce to simmer and simmer for 45 minutes. Add salt, and black and white pepper.

Partially whizz with a stick blender. I like green soup quite chunky, with pieces of potato and fennel, as well as the leaves themselves still being recognizable, but if you prefer your soups smooth just whizz for longer.

Potato is a great thickener in soups, as well as adding to the flavour, and it also helps make this soup quite substantial.

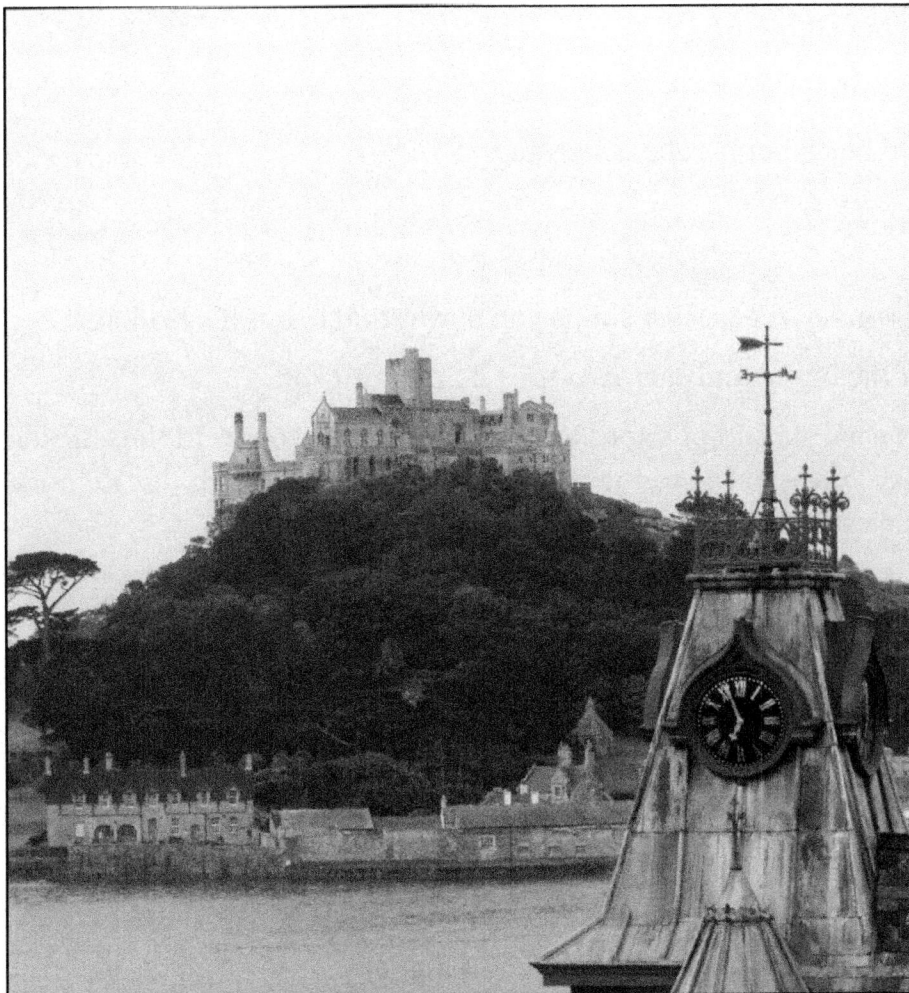

Marazion clock tower & St Michael's Mount

Lentil soup ▲

split red lentils, 150gm

chicken or vegetable stock, 1 litre

carrots, medium, 2, peeled, roughly chopped

onions, medium, 2, roughly chopped

potatoes, medium, 2, peeled, roughly chopped

bay leaves, 2

vegetable oil, 1 glug

salt to taste

ground black pepper, be generous!

4 portions

This is one of the easiest soups you'll ever make, but it's brilliant!

Sweat the onion and carrot in the oil and until soft.

Add the lentils and potatoes and stir to coat. Season. Add the chicken stock and bay leaves, bring to the boil and simmer for 40 minutes. Remove the bay leaves and whizz with a stick blender.

Very simple but very good.

Pheasant and watercress soup with orange, and garlic croutons

pheasant stock, 1 litre

orange zest, 2 tablespoons

watercress, 4 very good handfuls, stalks on, rough chopped

spring onions, 6, topped and tailed, sliced

groundnut oil, 4 glugs

salt, 2 pinches or more to taste

bread, white, 2 slices, crusts removed

garlic, 1 clove, peeled

2 portions

Add the oil to the soup pan over medium heat and when hot add half the spring onions and fry gently until soft and translucent, around 5 minutes. Add half the watercress and fry for 2 minutes before adding the stock.

Bring to the boil then add the orange zest, turn down and simmer for half an hour, then blitz with a stick blender to break up the onion and watercress and bring back to the simmer.

While the soup is gently simmering, heat a frying pan over a medium heat and when hot add the rest of the oil, when hot, gently place in the bread, dunking one side to get a coating of the oil, turn and fry until golden brown, then turn to fry the first side (it was dunked before frying in case all the oil was absorbed by the first side to be browned!). When both sides are golden brown remove and allow to cool before gently rubbing both sides with garlic. Now cut the bread into cubes (croutons) and set aside.

Add the remaining spring onions to the soup and simmer for 5 more minutes, remove from the heat and ladle into bowls. Sprinkle the remaining watercress over as a garnish, top off with the garlic croutons, take your delicious steaming creation and enjoy!

Simple mushroom soup

Any mushrooms; field, chestnut, button, portobello or a mix, work well here

mushrooms, large bowlful (equivalent of 6 large field mushrooms, yes lots!), finely chopped

1 ½ medium onions, finely chopped

garlic, 2 cloves, crushed

chicken or vegetable stock, 1 litre

goats' butter, 40 gm

salt & pepper to taste

4 large portions

Melt the butter in a large pan then sweat the onions and garlic for 5 minutes. Add 2/3 of the mushrooms and sweat for a further 5 minutes. Add the stock and simmer for 30 minutes. Add the remaining mushrooms, season and cook for 10 - 13 minutes.

Ladle this wonderful soup into bowls. A dash of chilli sherry makes this surprisingly special!

Chapel Point near Portmellon

Souper Trooter (gorgeous beetroot soup)

Prepare all the vegetables before you start to cook.

beetroot, around 500 gm pre-peeling, peeled, 0.5 cm sliced and cut into 2 cm pieces

onions, 2, peeled chopped

potato, medium, peeled, 0.5 cm sliced

chicken, duck or vegetable stock, 1.5 litres

celery, 1 stick, stringed, chopped

leek, 1, finely chopped

carrot 1 large, peeled & grated

Chinese or pointy cabbage, ½, chopped

fennel, 1 bulb, chopped

tomato purée, ⅓ tube

black pepper, good amount to taste

salt, 2 good pinches

red wine vinegar, 2 tablespoons

honey, 1 tablespoon

goats' butter, 1 good knob

vegetable oil, 3 glugs, to sweat the vegetables

yoghurt, plain, 4 tablespoons

Portions, 4

In a large stainless steel pan, place the beetroot and potatoes, add the stock, bring to boil, and simmer for 15 minutes. Remove the beetroot and potatoes with a slotted spoon and set the stock aside.

In the same pan, melt the butter or add the oil and heat. Add the onions celery, leek, fennel, and fry until softening - around 15 minutes. Add back the stock, bring to the boil and simmer for 5 minutes then add the carrot. Simmer further a further 5 minutes .

Colourful souper trooter finished with a swirl of goats' yoghurt

Add the cabbage, stir in the vinegar, honey, and tomato purée, and simmer for 10 minutes. Add back the beetroot and potatoes, and simmer for 5 minutes.

Partially whizz with a stick blender leaving some of the vegetables still chunky. Just use a food processor or liquidizer if you like it smooth!

Serve in bowls and top with yoghurt.

Spiced butternut soup

butternut squash, 1, peeled and cubed

potato, 1 medium, peeled and small cubed

onion, 1 large, chopped

carrot, 1 medium, chopped

garlic, 1 clove, finely chopped

ginger, 2 thumbs, unpeeled, chopped

sage, 20 leaves, stemmed removed, finely chopped

ground mace, ¼ tsp

vegetable stock, 1 litre

goats' butter, 1 knob

flavourless oil, glug

salt & pepper to taste

6 portions

Bring the vegetable stock to the boil, add the squash and simmer for 10 minutes then remove the squash and set aside.

Add the oil to a large pan over a medium heat then the butter. When the butter has melted add the onions, garlic, carrot, ginger, mace, sage and potato and sweat for 10 minutes. Add the reserved squash and stock and simmer for 30 minutes. Add salt and black pepper.

Whizz with a stick blender to preferred consistency.

Tomato & tarragon soup

ripe tomatoes, medium to large 10, sliced then chopped, woody bits removed

lemon, 1, juice of

green chilli, 1, no seeds, chopped

tarragon, 5 good sprigs, leaves chopped

chives, 1 good handful, chopped

chervil, including stalks, 1 good handful, chopped

good olive oil, 3 glugs

water, freshly boiled, 1 litre

Portions, 4

Heat the oil in a large saucepan over a medium heat and when hot add all the ingredients apart from the water, stir-fry for a few seconds to mix well before putting on a tight-fitting lid.

Stir-fry every two or three minutes to ensure all the ingredients are sweated. The tomatoes will give up their liquid quite quickly, turn the heat down so the liquid is simmering after 5 minutes.

Simmer for a further 10 minutes, then add the freshly boiled water and stir.

Simmer for a further 30 minutes then blitz with a stick blender and you're good to go!

Ladle into a couple of bowls and enjoy! This soup is also great cold, especially on a hot summer's day.

.

SALAD

Cucumber is versatile and not that tricky to grow

Dresses, flowers and leaves ▲

Catchy eh? Well I thought so!

Mayonnaise is a dressing after all! So it can be used to dress quite a few of the salads here, as well as being great mixed with egg or tuna and to make a prawn or crab cocktail. The flowers here bring wonderful colour to many dishes and are safe to eat and flavoursome, going well with many foods. The leaves page talks about a few leaves that you might not normally think about, as well as pods! Radish pods!

Mayonnaise

egg, the fresher the better, yolk, 1

vegetable, groundnut, or basic rapeseed oil, as much as it takes

good olive oil, or cold-pressed rapeseed oil, select flavour to go with the dish, as much as it takes

white wine vinegar, 2 dashes

salt to taste

all ingredients should be at room temperature

always use a glass or Pyrex bowl and I like to use a small metal whisk

2 portions. For more, increase the number of egg yolks and scale everything else up accordingly. By the way, this will be a wonderful golden yellow colour, not white!

First I'll take you through basic mayonnaise, which I prefer for coleslaw, or egg or tuna mayonnaise, for example, then I'll talk about how to alter flavours and additional ingredients depending on what the mayonnaise is to be used for.

Classic mayonnaise ingredients – egg yolks, extra virgin olive oil, vegetable oil, and salt

If your mayonnaise doesn't thicken don't worry! Sometimes the freshness of the eggs can cause a problem, and sometimes the air temperature or humidity on the day. Just have another go, making especially sure to use a cool clean bowl.

I like to save the egg whites, which are not needed in mayonnaise, for making meringues later. I keep adding them to a bag that I store in the freezer until there are enough. So, crack an egg over a pudding bowl to catch the white, keeping both halves facing upwards to ensure the yolk remains in one of the halves. Tip the white remaining in the other half into the now vacant half allowing any white remaining to fall into the bowl, and repeat to ensure most of the white is now in the pudding bowl.

Tip the yolk into a clean cool glass or Pyrex mixing bowl. If you notice much white remaining around the yolk dab it using a piece of kitchen towel to soak up as much as possible.

Now take a small whisk, or a fork if you like, and whisk the yolk for around a minute then add the white wine vinegar.

Now start to add a little of the less expensive oil and whisk until it is blended in, then a little more and blend again. Now add a little of the more expensive oil and blend, then a little more of the less expensive oil and blend again. And repeat again with the more expensive oil.

The amount of each oil added will determine the eventual flavour so reverse the quantities if you prefer the rapeseed or good olive oil flavour to be stronger.

Repeat the oil-adding steps, now adding more oil each time, but making sure all the oil is fully blended in before adding the next pouring.

Magically, the mayonnaise will thicken as you add more oil and you just need to keep going until it is as thick as you want it. Of course the volume will also increase, so everyone will have a little more!

I like mine very thick, almost being able to make it stand in peaks. In hot summers though, it won't thicken as much as in cooler weather. Now just add a sprinkling of salt to taste and stir it in.

Now for alternative flavour and ingredient ideas:

For mayonnaise to accompany green and potato salads, or to mix into a ranch (chopped) salad, a sprinkling of white pepper works well, while for dunking prawns a squeeze of lemon, or lemon and a clove of crushed garlic are excellent.

If you're making mayonnaise for salad, you could also try reversing the quantities of the oils; additional olive oil will add pepperiness. You can also make a really tasty asparagus mayonnaise by adding the heads of around 10 lightly steamed spears.

For egg mayonnaise add 4 chopped just hard-boiled eggs along with a little extra salt and white pepper.

Tomato is a great flavour to add to egg mayonnaise: to make it, take 2 large ripe tomatoes, slice them in half and squeeze the juice and seeds into a bowl and store in the fridge for using later. Then slice and dice the tomato halves, remove the woody bits, and slide the tomato pieces into the egg mayonnaise, add a little more salt, and stir. I love it in soft bread rolls or on crackers!

Portion control here is through the number of egg yolks and quantity of oil added. Generally though 1 egg yolk = 2 portions, with everything else scaled around it! 2 egg yolk will magically generate 4 portions. Somehow this works whether you're making a side dressing for a salad, a potato salad, coleslaw, or even tuna mayonnaise using a tin of tuna (in spring water, drained and well squeezed using the lid to extract the water).

Edible flowers

Nasturtiums are really easy to grow and in greenhouses they grow right through the winter. Better still they come in all kinds of colours. The flowers are peppery so add flavour as well as a great visual boost to a salad plate – either as individual petals or whole flowers.

Borage flowers not only have a great look, but at first taste are surprisingly "cucumbery"!

Mustard flowers, on the left, a lovely bright yellow, add a touch of mustardy heat to your salads, whilst marigold or calendula petals look just fabulous scattered among the greenery of your salad leaves. Both are easy to grow at home. They'll sometimes grow year round in a greenhouse.

Radish pods are quite brilliant, not quite flowers and not quite leaves! They are crunchy and juicy and have a great radish flavour, they can be a bit variable in heat. The best thing is that you get loads of them per plant! Just let them grow. The plants flower, then produce delicious pods. For a continuous crop sow a few seeds every 3 to 4 weeks.

Wild garlic is a terrific find. This is a woodland variety; you can find the leaves in the spring, then flowering late in spring. The flowers add a nice dash to a bowl of green salad leaves. Hedgerow wild garlic is also fabulous, grows from November, with white flowers in spring similar in shape to bluebells. It has long narrow leaves. There is also a pink flowering variety of wild garlic which is rare but amazing if you can find it.

Cornflowers look great on the plate adding wonderful colour. They are sweet and a little spicy.

Leaves

Here are some more ideas to broaden the flavour of your salad bowl. It's great that it's not too difficult to find multiple types of lettuce for your salads today, but here are a few of the leaves Mamá grows that I like to use to bring a bit more zing to a salad.

Watercress is surprisingly easy to grow at home and believe it or not does NOT need to be planted in or near to water! It grows well in dark shady spots where many plants just do not get on. If you get the spot right it grows quickly too.

Watercress leaves, left, add a lovely zing to a bowl of mixed leaves, bringing heat, sometime a strong hint of pepper, and darker green shades.

Basil leaves, below, add a unique freshness to a mixed salad bowl, and are a lovely addition to a tomato salad too. (Shouldn't be saying this here, but they're also a wonderful addition to a tomato omelette!)

Mustard leaves have lots of flavour but can be quite hot. Best to tear them into smaller pieces rather than leave them whole when adding them to your salads. A wide range of mustard varieties can be easily grown at home, outside or in the greenhouse. Why not try a few, for their different colours!

When we think nasturtium most of us think of the fantastically colourful flowers, but give the leaves a chance. They are lovely and peppery and can be quite crispy, The leaves are best eaten when they're medium sized rather than larger and older. Test them for pepperiness before deciding whether or not to rip them into smaller pieces before adding them to your salad bowl.

Sorrel is a wonderful leaf, similar to lettuce in looks, but with a tangy lemon flavour. it goes well as a salad leaf adding a wow taste of citrus to the bowl. Shouldn't be saying this here, but if you take out the centre veins and tear half a dozen large leaves they go really well in an omelette! It's easy to grow, outside or in the greenhouse, and it regrows every year.

Artichoke and garlic salad ▲

Artichoke hearts, 1 tin (around 400g, drained and dried

garlic, 3 cloves, peeled, fine chopped

very good olive oil, 3 good glugs

vinegar, white wine, 2 teaspoons

salt, 1 pinch

4 portions

Dead easy to prepare, it needs a minimum of 1 hour prior to eating for the flavours to meld. It is also very good after hours and hours, so you can make it well in advance of the meal if you like.

Simply halve the artichoke hearts and put them into a shallow bowl or deep plate with slightly raised sides, sprinkle the garlic over and mix together, then sprinkle the salt, the oil and the vinegar over and turn well.

Just leave for a minimum of one hour for the flavours to meld, re-turning every 15 minutes until you are ready to take to the table.

Asparagus salad ▲

asparagus spears, fresh, 12

garlic, ½ clove, very finely chopped

good olive oil, 1 glug

2 portions

A perfect 'taster' dish to add to any full salad meal. Lots of flavours in small dishes to accompany the main salad event are great. They don't take long to prepare, and add splendid variety to any salad table.

With this salad, the key is avoid "over-garlicking" the asparagus. You just want a hint of garlic. So, just break off the woody bits of the asparagus spears, setting them aside for making stock later – freeze them if you've no immediate asparagus soup plans – then place the spears into an already steaming steamer for just 5 minutes.

Remove from the steamer, place in a shallow bowl and sprinkle the garlic and oil over, turn together gently and leave for 5 - 10 minutes. Now, take a kitchen towel and very gently wipe the spears to remove the garlic. You'll be left with lovely crunchy asparagus with hints of the peppery oil and garlic – a great combination.

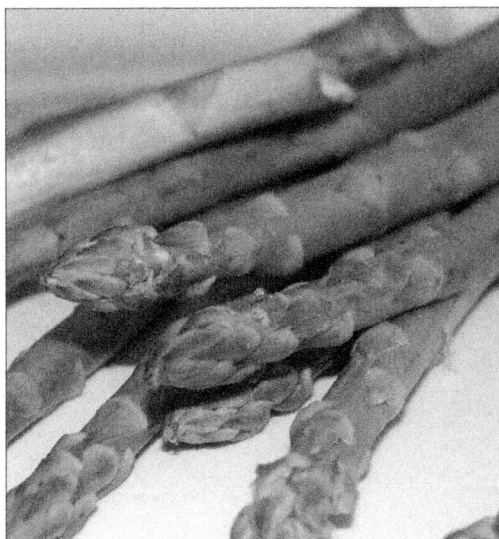

Fowey blockhouse with Gribbin Head daymark in the distance, across Fowey estuary from the Polruan blockhouse.

The blockhouses were built in the 1300s and a chain was strung between them. Normally resting on the bed of the estuary, it was raised to keep undesirable ships out of the harbour!

Beef - (warm) salad with mushrooms and watercress

Sirloin steaks, ½ kilo

watercress, 2 good handfuls

mushrooms, 2, chestnut, large, sliced

honey mustard dressing (1 glug good olive oil, pinch of salt, juice of half a lemon, 1½ teaspoons French wholegrain mustard, 1 tspn of white wine vinegar, 2 tspns of runny honey, whisked). Taste and adjust as you like!

groundnut oil, 1 glug

2 portions

I just love watercress, and I think the combination of warm pink steak and watercress is fantastic. But, I know that some people aren't so keen on watercress and like their meat well cooked, so feel free to add rocket or lettuce or other leaves to the salad, and cook the steak as you like it.

Prepare the honey mustard dressing first.

Prepare the watercress by just snapping off the woodier pieces of stem, then simply wash and dry. Now put a griddle, or frying pan if you haven't got a griddle, over a medium to high heat and when almost, but not quite, blue smokey hot brush the steaks with oil, sprinkle a little salt over and put them oil side down on the griddle / in the pan.

Cook to your own satisfaction; Cook for around 4 minutes on each side for medium rare, depending how thick the steak is; around 3 minutes on each side will leave your steak rare and 5 minutes, well done. Don't forget to oil and salt the other side of the steaks before you turn them. If the steak are particularly thick, add a minute per side.

While the steak is cooking prepare the salad by adding the watercress and mushrooms to two bowls. When the steak is cooked, slice thinly, add to the bowls and toss. Finally sprinkle the dressing over lavishly and take to the table while the beef is still warm.

Beef - sirloin steak - salad, with watercress, rocket, and spicy citrus dressing, with freshly grated Parmesan or Pecorino ▲

sirloin steak, ½ kilo

lemons, 3

orange, 1

chilli, fresh, small red, 1, chopped with seeds, or 2 mild home grown purple chillies

watercress, 2 good handfuls

rocket, 2 good handfuls

spinach leaves, 1 handful

lettuce, cos, a few leaves

balsamic vinegar, 2 glugs

roasted sesame oil, 2 glugs

garlic, 1 clove, peeled and crushed

salt, 1 good pinch

goats' butter, 1 knob

good olive oil, 1 glug

Pecorino or Parmesan cheese, 2 - 3 tablespoons, freshly grated

2 portions

First make a marinade with the juice of the orange and lemons, chilli, garlic, sesame oil, balsamic vinegar and salt, allow to meld for 15 minutes. Thinly slice the steak (around 4mm) and soak in the marinade for 1 hour, then remove the steak and set aside.

Now we're going to turn the marinade into the spicy citrus dressing. Simply put it into a small saucepan with the butter, and reduce by half.

While this is happening, make up the leaf salad, and assemble on two plates.

Put frying pan or wok over a medium heat and allow to get very hot before adding the oil. When the olive oil is very hot add the steak slices and stir-fry, turning every 10 - 15 seconds. If you like your steak pink, stir-fry for just 20 - 30 seconds. Well-done will take 60 - 70 seconds or so and medium 40 - 50 seconds.

Now place the steak slices on the salad leaves and drizzle the spicy citrus dressing over. Finish the dish by sprinkling the Parmesan or Pecorino cheese, over and serve immediately.

The hot dressing nicely wilts the leaves and the spiciness adds a new dimension to them. The cheese seasons.

Sea views from a field at Treen

Celeriac salad cubes ▲

Celeriac, 1

Good olive oil, 4 good slugs

Salt, 2 teaspoons

4 portions

Peel the celeriac, making sure you don't leave any skin or roots attached; but don't take off too much of the flesh. A potato peeler will take off much of the skin and a carefully applied sharp knife will take off the rooty bits.

Carefully slice the celeriac into 15mm slices, as evenly thick as possible across each slice. Because celeriac is so hard they are quite tough to cut through so be VERY careful that the knife and celeriac don't slip while you are cutting as it will be quite easy to cut yourself if you are not! You will probably end up with 5 or 6 fritters. Scrunch sea salt over one side.

Heat two frying pans over medium heat and when hot add the olive oil. It should be around 5mm deep. When the oil is hot add 2 or 3 fritters to each pan, salted side down; they should start sizzling straight away.

Simply fry them for around 10 minutes, after which the cooked side of the fritters should be golden brown. Don't worry if they are beginning to blacken in places.

Salt the top sides of the fritters then turn them and fry for around another 10 minutes until golden brown on the other side. Test for cookedness with a knife or fork, they should still be little al dente. If you'd like them softer leave for a little longer. Remove from pan, put aside and leave to go cold.

Simply cut the fritters into 15mm squares so you end up with cubes, and serve as a mini salad. What a surprise!

Chicken, summer salad with balsamic mustard dressing and mayonnaise

chicken, cooked, whole, cold, portions carved to suit

tomatoes, plum, vine, small, 8 – sliced, woody bits removed

salt, 2 - 3 good pinches

olive oil, best, 1 good glug

radishes, 10, with a few radish pods if you can get them (grow your own, but don't harvest them. They will flower, then produce crispy pods which are delicious. The Victorians loved them!!)

potato salad, 2 portions

lettuce leaves, romaine, crisp, 8

watercress, 1 handful

rocket, ideally, ne good handful (or two, if you love it like I do)

balsamic mustard dressing (1 glug good olive oil, pinch of salt, juice of half a lemon, 1½ teaspoons French wholegrain mustard, glug of good balsamic vinegar, whisked)

2 portions

Place the tomatoes, spread evenly, on a plate and scrunch a couple of pinches of sea salt over, then drizzle with the olive oil. Leave for 30 minutes to let the flavours permeate.

Make up the balsamic mustard dressing. Make up the mayonnaise.

Tear the lettuce into medium sized pieces and put in a medium bowl, put radishes and rocket on top and pour the dressing over. Toss until the dressing coats the salad evenly.

Slice a few pieces of chicken breast, put on the plates, then arrange the tomato salad next to it. Now add the green and potato salads, set the mayonnaise on the side and........enjoy!

Duck - crispy and shredded with tomato salad

duck breasts, 2

Tamari soy sauce or balsamic vinegar, 2 good glugs

tomatoes, medium, 4

shallot, 1, peeled and chopped

salt, 2 pinches

garlic, 1 clove, peeled and finely chopped

fresh basil leaves, 12

good olive oil, 2 good glugs

groundnut oil, 1 glug

2 portions

First switch on the oven to preheat to 200°C, 180°C fan, then prepare the duck breasts by scoring them deeply on both sides. Now put them in a shallow bowl and drizzle 2 glugs of Tamari soy sauce or balsamic vinegar over and massage in, making sure you get the soy or balsamic deep into the scores. Now add a pinch of salt, spreading evenly over the breasts and set aside for 10 minutes.

For the salad, thinly slice the tomatoes and remove the woody bits, place in a salad bowl. Add the garlic, shallot, a pinch of salt, a good glug of Tamari soy sauce or balsamic vinegar, the basil leaves and a good glug of olive oil then toss and set aside for the flavours to meld – don't eat this salad for at least 20 minutes after preparing it, and re-toss every 10 minutes or so.

While the salad is busy melding, you're going to fry the duck, so place a frying pan or griddle over a medium heat and when hot add the groundnut oil (but not if using the griddle, brush the oil onto the duck instead). When the oil is hot add the duck breasts and fry on each side for around 5 minutes, remove and allow to cool so that you can touch them without burning yourself. Now remove the skin and shred the duck by gently teasing the fibres apart between your thumbs and forefingers, placing the shredded duck onto a plate.

Now place a baking tray in the oven and get it good and hot, then remove it from the oven, place the duck on it, spread it about, and then replace the tray in the oven. After 5 minutes turn the duck, and after 20 minutes it should be nice and crispy, so remove it from the oven.

Assemble the salad on 2 plates and carefully place the duck on top – this looks and tastes fantastic and is quite a different kind of salad!

Free ranging ducks ruling the roost on a gorgeous day in Cornwall.

Leek and chicory salad ▲

leek, 1, topped and tailed and thinly sliced

chicory, 1, outer leaves removed, thinly sliced

balsamic vinegar, 1 glug (try Tamari soy sauce if you or your guests have sensitivities to balsamic vinegar)

salt, 1 teaspoon

4 portions

This, like the other salads in this section, is intended as a lively side show to the main element of a salad, to add variety to the range of tastes and textures so they set one another off. So, smallish portions are the order of the day.

Steam the leek and chicory until softened but still with a bit of crunch – just keep taking the odd piece and tasting until they're ready. It should take only around 4 - 6 minutes depending on how thin the slices are. Then remove from the steamer and lay on kitchen towel and pat dry.

Finally lay in a shallow bowl and drizzle with the balsamic, toss, sprinkle the salt over and it's done.

Mushrooms with soy salad ▲

button mushrooms, 12, finely sliced

Tamari soy sauce, a light sprinkling (½ a glug)

4 portions

One of the easiest salads you'll ever make and an interesting sideshow to the main salad event, adding variety and flavours to the meal.

Fresh chestnut mushrooms looking good before 'cooking' in the soy

Simply slice the mushrooms from top to bottom thinly and place them on a shallow dish. Sprinkle the soy over, toss and spread them around the plate evenly. If the mushrooms seem a little dry after ½ an hour sprinkle more soy over.

Fantastic combination of flavours in this one, the mushrooms actually partially cook in the soy and will shrink in size as this happens. Best eaten after leaving to meld for an hour or so. Also great on pizza

Potato salad ▲

potatoes, medium, 3, peeled, chopped into bite sized pieces

mayonnaise, 2 portions, see my recipe on page 44

Portions, 2

Put the potatoes into a medium sized saucepan and add water until it is just covering them.

Over a medium heat bring the pan to the boil and allow to boil for 2 minutes before turning off the heat. Leave the potatoes in the hot water where they will cook in the residual heat.

Leave the potatoes in the water and by the time the water is cold the potatoes will be cooked!

Not too hard, not too soft, and they won't break up.

Drain the potatoes through a sieve and with a slotted spoon lay them on a piece of kitchen towel and pat dry.

Now simply tip the potatoes into the mayonnaise and stir gently, and there you have a simple potato salad.

Ranch or chopped salad ⛺

potatoes, medium, 2 peeled and 1½ cm diced

little gem lettuce, 1, shredded

celery, 2 sticks, stringed and chopped

tomatoes, medium, 2 chopped

cucumber, 10cm, 4in, peeled, seeded and chopped

radishes, 4, small diced

mayonnaise (see page 44), 4 tbspns

4 portions

Bring the potatoes to the boil, simmer for 2 minutes then turn off the heat and leave the pan to cool. The potatoes will cook in the residual heat but, crucially, they will not break up. When cool, drain and set aside to dry.

Then just mix everything together in a glass bowl. A very simple, crunchy, salad with the strong individual salad ingredient flavours coming through.

Mevagissey lighthouse from the SW coast path.

STUFF

Stuff?

What's stuff? You might ask.

Well, it's spoon and fork food;
stuff you can eat with your fingers;
sofa stuff; picnic stuff; beach stuff;
camping stuff. There's vegetable
stuff, meat & poultry stuff,
fish & seafood;
sea stuff.

Sea

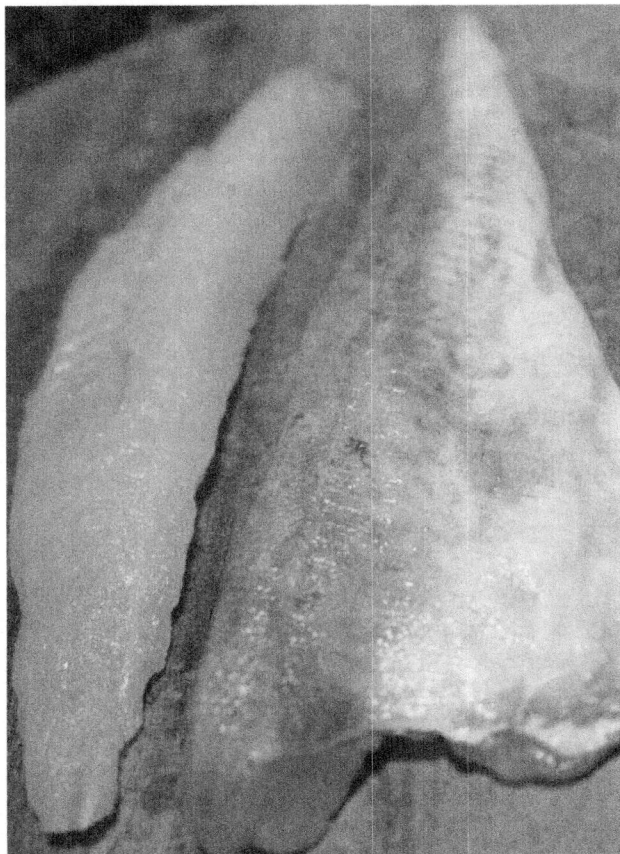

I love fish, and for some dishes the skin is best removed. Your fishmonger will do it, but in case you didn't ask, here's how. (The picture, bottom left, will help).

I've used Red Gurnard for the example here, it's great value, amazingly tasty and absolutely gorgeous poached with chervil, with a poached egg, for breakfast (see page 86).

Press the very end of the tail of the fillet tight to the board with your thumb nail. Hold knife in position shown, cut down into fillet against and in front of your thumb nail, knife blade sloping away from you, and cut along the skin 2 cm. Then lift skin between thumb and forefinger, as shown, keeping forefinger pressed down to board and continue cutting along skin, knife blade sloping. After 5 cm move your grip 5 cm along leaving the knife where it is with blade pressed to skin, grip tightly and continue cutting. Repeat until you've skinned the whole fillet.

Crab - creamy coriander crab sauce with pappardelle

crabmeat, white, 2 good handfuls (around 150gm)

crabmeat, brown, 1 cupful (around 100gm). Use the orange roe (eggs) too if you have any. It has loads of flavour, stays whole and adds visual impact to the finished dish (see overleaf). Use white meat to make up the quantity if insufficient brown meat

shallots, banana, 4, peeled & small chopped (ordinary shallots, or onions will be fine if you can't get banana shallots)

garlic, 7 large cloves, crushed

dried chillies, ½ teaspoon, or other type or quantity to taste

coriander, fresh, include stalks, chopped, good handful (around 10 gm)

tomatoes, cherry, 14, woody bits removed, chopped – use seeds & all

mushrooms, button, large, 5, chopped

sherry, dry, 1 slug

crab stock, 1 mugful. Use water if can't get or make crab stock (page 17)

double cream or Oat cream, 1 slug

good olive oil, 1 glug

salt to taste

egg pappardelle or any long pasta, can be gluten-free, 350 gm

4 portions

I first made this dish just after getting a call from my local fishmonger to say she had managed to get spider crabs in for me. Because many British fishermen throw them overboard (unless catching to order for the French or Spanish!), they are not that easy to come by in this country – so I have an open request with Kim to get me a couple in when she can, and it is always a joy to get that call out of the blue.

Brown crabs will also go well in this dish, but I really like the extra sweetness of the spiders. For the quantities of meat required you'll probably need 2 medium sized spiders, or 1 – 2 brown crabs. If your crabs are live when you get them, pop them in the freezer for 30 minutes to make them sleepy then into a large pan of boiling water for just 10 – 15 minutes once the water is back to the boil, depending on size, then take them out and leave to cool on a rack.

Delicious and colourful creamy crab sauce with pappardelle pasta

Total cooking time is around 1½ hours, but you should also allow around 30 minutes to an hour for picking the crabmeat, especially if you've been lucky enough to get spiders – they are much tougher than brown crabs; use a rubber mallet to get into the claws, or the back of a very heavy knife, and nut crackers for the legs. Use the small end of a small teaspoon to prise the meat from the legs.

Don't bash or squeeze the claws and legs too hard – you're aiming to get a crack that you can prise open, or you'll end up with smashed shell in the meat which takes time to pick out. With a glass of wine to accompany, this part of the prep can be really relaxing believe it or not; I love it. There's also the chef's treat of tasting the crabmeat of course!

Pappardelle is wide flat pasta, which just seems to go really well with this dish, but other pastas would also be suitable if you can't get it.

Heat a large saucepan pan over low to medium heat then add olive oil. When hot add shallots, chilli and garlic; fry lightly until translucent (around 5 minutes).

Add the brown crabmeat, three quarters of the coriander, tomatoes, and half the stock / water; bring to the boil and simmer for 30 minutes; test for heat after 15 minutes and add more chilli if you want it hotter. Stir every 5 minutes to stop it sticking.

Then add mushrooms and sherry and simmer for 45 minutes stirring every 10 minutes, keeping an eye on how dry the sauce is.

You're aiming for the consistency of double cream – not watery, but not so dry the sauce doesn't run and coat the pasta when it is poured on. Add more stock / water, and make use of the pan lid to partially cover to retain moisture as needed.

Bring the pasta water to the boil, add loads of salt, then the pappardelle and stir to make sure it doesn't stick to the bottom of the pan.

Add the white crabmeat and cream to the sauce and stir in lightly. You're aiming to keep the chunkiness of the meat as far as possible rather than breaking it up.

By the time the pasta is cooked (probably another 6 - 7 minutes, but read the instructions on the packet) the sauce will have been bought back to the simmer so the dish will be ready to serve.

Lay the pasta in the bottom of warmed bowls, spoon the sauce over, sprinkle the remaining coriander over and enjoy.

Razor clams with sorrel sauce

razor clams, 6, washed

onion, medium, 1, chopped (or use 2 shallots instead)

garlic, 2 cloves, crushed

cream, double or Oat cream, 1 good slug

white wine, not too dry, 4 good slugs

sorrel, 12 large leaves, main stalks removed, sliced

good olive oil, 2 good slugs

salt to taste

Portions 2

Once the clams are cooked and eaten you'll have sauce left over and it can be used really well with other fish dishes - when I tried it with crabcakes and fishcakes it was delicious.

Add the oil to a hot large saucepan that has a well-fitting lid, add the onion and garlic and fry off on medium heat until they are soft. Add the clams and wine, put the lid on the pan and shake it well.

After 6 minutes add the cream and sorrel, then simmer for another 10 minutes.

Simple – remove the clams, cut off and the bulbous end and thinner bit, then serve with as much sauce as you like.

These clams are great cold or chilled.

Crab pasty with spicy stir-fried bean sprouts

crabmeat, white, 2 large cupfuls (meat from 6 - 8 medium sized claws)

tomatoes, cherry, 8, cut in half

potatoes, 2 medium, peeled, cubed, soaked in water for 1 hour

spring onions, large, 6, diagonally sliced into large chunks

crispy butter pastry, 300 gm, rolled into 2 discs, 22cm – 25cm, see my recipe on page 152, reducing quantities by 1/3

egg, 1, beaten

crab stock, ½ litre

small chillies, 2, seeds in, chopped

garlic, 3 cloves, chopped

coriander, fresh, 1 good handful, rough chopped

lime juice from ½ lime

salt, good pinch

kaffir lime leaves, or lemon or lime leaves, 4

cornflour, 1 teaspoon

water, 1 tablespoon

bean sprouts, 1 handful, soaked in cold salted water for 1 hour

2 portions

Take the shells and claws from your crab to make the stock, using standard ingredients - onion, bay leaves, peppercorns, and carrot and water, simmered for around one and a half hours. Eight medium claws should be enough, or a whole shell, with legs and claws. Use fish stock if you can't make crab stock.

Colourful ingredients, all add up to a thoroughly tasty crab pasty!

When the stock is ready you're ready to make the sauce. Put the stock into a medium sized pan, add the chillies, coriander, lime leaves, salt and garlic, begin reducing to around 1 cupful. Mix the cornflour with the water, remove the sauce reduction from the heat, add the cornflour mix, stir briskly and thoroughly. Now bring back to the heat and continue to stir until the sauce has thickened and set the sauce aside.

Now make the pastry, following the recipe on page 152 but using only 2/3 of the ingredients weights and quantities , and while it is resting in the fridge for half an hour prepare the pasty filling as described above.

Now turn on the oven and preheat to 190ºC, 170ºC Fan.

The rolling of the pastry and forming into pasties is, as those of you who have made glute- free pastry before will know, not as straight forward as making pastry, pasties and pies using flour containing gluten. That's because gluten-free flour doesn't contain the "glue" that keeps most pastry together, helps it to stretch and makes it relatively easy to work and fold.

So, for those of you that haven't made and worked with glute- free dough before this could be a bit of an adventure!

After removing the dough from the fridge and leaving it to warm for 5 minutes, split it into two. Form each half into a ball by rolling softly between the palms of your hands. Take one of the balls and roll it around a well-floured piece of baking parchment 32 cm square, re-flour the WHOLE of the rest of the parchment.

Now press down on the ball with the palm of one hand until it is around 3 – 4 cm, thick. Sprinkle more flour over the dough, rub flour over the rolling pin, and sprinkle plenty more flour every two passes of the roller, rolling out to around 26 cm, diameter circles. Don't worry if your finished circle is a bit "ovally"!

If the pastry ends up over the edge of the parchment just use the pallet knife to trim it back until the pastry edge is 1 cm or so inside the parchment. Set the cuttings aside, keeping them flat, until the pasty is assembled as you might need it for patching, which would be normal. No cuttings? Don't worry, you'll have some if you need them once you've folded over your pasty top!

First, take one of the portions of crabmeat and place it in a half-moon shape on the left of your pasty, around 2½ cm from the edges, sprinkle lightly with salt. Now take one portion of potato and spread it between the crabmeat and just to the left of the centre line of the pastry same distance from the pastry edges, sprinkle lightly with salt. Then sprinkle half the spring onions over the crabmeat and potatoes, and finally sprinkle the chopped tomatoes over as a top layer and sprinkle lightly with salt. The right side of the potato should be just short of hallway across your circle.

Use a pastry brush to lightly brush the flour away from the edges of your circle and off the parchment, avoiding disturbing it's edges.

To begin the folding over of the pasty top, gently raise the parchment underneath the unfilled half with your left hand so that you can slide your right hand, palm side up, underneath until the pastry is firmly resting on the palm of your hand, with the edge of your right hand firmly butting up against the line of swede. Remove your left hand from the parchment.

Now, smoothly and fairly swiftly, flip your right hand over and leftwards taking the parchment and pastry with it so that they fold over the filling with the unfilled edge sitting as closely as possible over the filled edge. If the fit isn't exact don't worry.

Gently peel back the parchment and lay it flat. Trim round the pastry edges and use the trimmings to patch any holes revealed when the parchment was pulled back, gently tapping them into place. Don't try to crimp the top and bottom edges together, just press them together gently. They will seal well during cooking.

Now carefully, holding the left and right edges of the parchment, lift it with the pasty onto your baking tray and cut off with scissors the half not containing the pasty.

Now repeat with the second pasty and finally trim any parchment overhanging the baking tray with scissors to prevent it burning, brush the pasties with the beaten egg and lift your tray into the preheated oven.

Leave until the pasties are a golden brown which will be after around 45 minutes. 10 minutes before the pasties are ready, begin stir-frying the bean sprouts in a wok with a small amount of vegetable oil and after 2 minutes add the sauce and continue stir-frying for around 4 minutes when the sauce will be ready.

Now just serve and savour the delicate pasty flavours alongside the spiciness of the sauce.

If you like, to add more flavour you could add sesame oil to the sauce or stir-fry the bean sprouts in sesame oil instead of vegetable oil.

Crab sauce

shellfish stock, 250 ml

onion, 1 medium, finely chopped

tomatoes, 6 skinned, seeded and small diced

button mushrooms, 6-8 small diced

white crabmeat, 2 handfuls

brown crabmeat, 1 handful

lemon, 1/4 juice of

dry sherry, 1 tspn (optional)

goats' butter, 1 knob

flavourless oil, 1 glug

salt & black pepper to taste

4 portions

In a pan, fry the onion in butter and oil until soft 10-15 minutes. Add the tomato and mushroom and sweat for a further 10 minutes. Add the stock and lemon juice and simmer for 5 minutes then whizz with a stick blender to break up but not leave smooth.

Add the crabmeat and sherry if using and simmer for 5 minutes. Season.

Great with pasta or as the base for a crab bake with the addition of some oat cream or goat's or sheep's yoghurt into the reduced and thickened sauce and a breadcrumb and chopped chervil topping.

Curried crab cakes with lemon and watercress mayonnaise and tomato

crabmeat, white, around 170 gm

new potatoes, 12, boiled and squished

garam masala, 1 dspn

egg, 1

cardamoms, 8, whole, skinned, chopped

tomatoes, 2, halved

mayonnaise, 2 eggs worth - see page 44

watercress, chopped, 1 good handful

lemon, ½

vegetable oil, 2 glugs

portions, 4 (2 cakes per portion)

This will make 8 cakes; around 7.5 cm diameter by 2 cm deep.

To make the cakes simply add the crabmeat to the potatoes, sprinkle the curry masala over then add the egg and mix together well.

Make up the mayonnaise before you begin the cake mix, adding the watercress and lemon juice just before you start cooking the cakes.

Add the chopped cardamoms and oil to a frying pan and heat over a moderate heat so the cardamom flavour infuses, and when hot, add the cakes, and the tomatoes. You may need two frying pans.

Cook for just 3 minutes before turning to cook for another two minutes. Plate up the cakes and tomatoes. Serve with the mayonnaise. Great for a light lunch.

Mevagissey mystic spider crab bake

spider crabmeat, white and brown, 500gm

mushrooms, button, medium, 6, sliced

shallots, 4, fine chopped

goats' butter, 2 good knobs

eggs, 2

double cream or Oat cream, 80 ml

crème fraîche, 100 ml

horseradish sauce, 1 tablespoon

dry sherry, 1 good glug

parmesan or pecorino, grated, 1 cup

parsley, fresh, chopped, 1 good handful

breadcrumbs, fresh, white, 3 good handfuls

Worcestershire sauce, 4 glugs or Tamari soy sauce, 2 glugs

black pepper to taste, at least 6 good grinds

spider crab shells for serving, 2

4 portions

Spider crab has amazing flavour, much sweeter than red or brown crab and well worth the extra effort with the rolling pin or rubber mallet to extract the wonderful meat from the spectacularly reinforced legs and shell.

Spiders can be difficult to find in the shops as we apparently don't eat them here in the UK so most that are landed here end up trucking it to Spain and France. A friendly word in the ear of a local crab fisherman or fresh fish stallholder on the quay can get you a couple to order though.

Crab bake in stunning spider crab shells

If you're preparing your own crab, allow at least 30 minutes to extract all the meat, and make sure you have a sturdy wooden board to hand and a solid wooden rolling pin to crack open the legs and body shell. Keep the shell for baking, use two shells for the four portions this recipe will make.

This dish is based on ideas I got from a recipe originating in Mystic, Connecticut, for a crab dip, made more substantial for a main meal.

Beat the eggs hard until frothy and set aside, then mix the white and brown spider crabmeat together in a mixing bowl, add the pepper then half the breadcrumbs and parsley and stir well. Melt 1 knob of butter in a frying pan, then add the shallots and mushrooms, frying gently and stirring occasionally until soft. Remove from the pan and set aside.

Add the cream and crème fraîche to a small bowl and mix well until you have the beginnings of a creamy sauce, then add half the parmesan or pecorino and horseradish and stir in. Add the remaining knob of butter to the frying pan and when melted add the sauce mix and stir, then add the sherry. Beat the eggs again to lighten a little more then add 3 tablespoons of the sauce to the eggs and stir in, then add the egg mix to the pan and stir well – just for 30 seconds or so as you don't want the egg to cook, just to thicken the sauce a little.

Now add the sauce to the crab mix and stir well, pour the mixture into a shallow baking dish or two spider crab shells (this is ideal because you get the incredible aroma from the baking shells as the dish cooks) so you have a depth of around 25 - 40 mm. In a small bowl mix the remaining breadcrumbs parmesan and parsley then sprinkle over the crab mix.

Put in a preheated oven at around 180ºC for 30 minutes (have a look after 20 minutes just to check, and if ready by then remove) by which time the crust will be golden brown, remove and serve immediately.

Mevagissey harbour

Monkfish & tiger prawns in spiced tomato and coriander sauce

monkfish, cleaned, 200g, cut into bite sized pieces

tiger prawns, uncooked, shelled, 20

fish stock, 1 litre, see page 83 for recipe

coconut milk, 250ml

goats' butter, unsalted, 100g

coriander, ground, 1 tablespoon

coriander, fresh, chopped (with stalks), 1 handful

garam masala, 2 tablespoons

mace, 4 small pieces

cardamoms, green, whole, 10

onions, medium - large, 3, peeled & chopped

garlic, 4 cloves, peeled, finely chopped

tomatoes, medium, 6, chopped, woody bits removed

salt, to taste

2 Portions

Begin by starting to reduce the fish stock to around 2/3 the volume.

Put the garam masala and ground coriander into a cup or small bowl, add around 4 - 5 tablespoons of cold water and stir, mixing the powdered spices into a smooth paste.

Heat a medium pan, add the butter, when melted and bubbling, add the paste, cardamoms and mace. Fry for 7 - 8 minutes, stirring occasionally, then add the onions and garlic and fry for 10 minutes stirring frequently, before adding the tomatoes. Turn heat to low, partially cover with lid and simmer for 30 minutes.

Add fish stock and coconut milk and continue to simmer for another hour to hour and 15 minutes, stirring every 5 minutes or so with a flat ended wooden spoon to stop the mixture sticking to the bottom of the pan. The mixture should be at the final consistency required before the next stage so if it doesn't look as though it will get there in time take off the lid so that it reduces more quickly.

(If the dish is overly saucy when finished don't worry, the leftover sauce will go well with pasta or a baked potato as a light lunch or starter!)

Add the monkfish pieces and continue to simmer for 10 minutes then add the prawns and fresh coriander, stirring in carefully but well.

Simmer for 5 more minutes and you're ready to serve with basmati rice.

Fantastic hand-crafted flags surround Mevagissey harbour during feast week

Popcorn prawns ▲

prawns, small, cooked, shelled, 3 good handfuls

flour, plain, 100gm

oat milk, 250ml

sweet paprika, 2 tbspn

salt, 2 good pinches

black pepper, ground, ½ - 1 tspn

lemon, ½ juice of

vegetable oil, 2 glugs

Portions , 2

This is a wonderful snack and not too time consuming to make but you do have to be prepared to be patient - the marinade takes a day or two!

You're going to marinade the prawns in the oat milk and lemon juice overnight or longer in the fridge, a couple of days is great.

Heat the oat milk until it is very warm then remove from the heat and add the lemon juice and a pinch of salt. Allow to cool and pour into a food bag.

Now drop the prawns into the bag, tie it or seal it tightly and place it in the fridge. Marinade for at least 18 hours, and up to 48 hours is great.

Mix together the flour, another good pinch of salt, paprika and pepper on a plate, take the prawns from the bag and shake to remove excess moisture then drop onto the plate and toss in the flour mix to coat them all over.

Add the oil to a frying pan and place over a medium to high heat. When hot gently place the prawns in the pan and they will begin their sizzle! After 3 or 4 minutes the prawns will be browning so turn them, fry them for just a minute or two more and they will be ready!

Now just use a slotted spoon to scoop them out and onto your snack plates, try them and wish you'd marinaded more!!

Red gurnard poached with chervil, with poached egg

gurnard fillets 15cm – 20cm long, skinned, 2

eggs, 2

fresh chervil, chopped, 1 handful

extra virgin olive oil, 2 glugs

salt, 2 pinches

white wine vinegar, 4 shakes

portions, 2, with 1 fillet and 1 egg per portion

Note that the gurnard is poached in boiling water in an ordinary plastic freezer bag, using 1 small bag for 2 fillets, 2 bags for 4, and so on. To make it easier to take the fillets out of the poaching bag without spoiling their look, have a pair of scissors and a pallet knife or long thin spatula to hand! Also, have the poaching bag laying near your board and opened, ready for your fish to gently slide into, before you start.

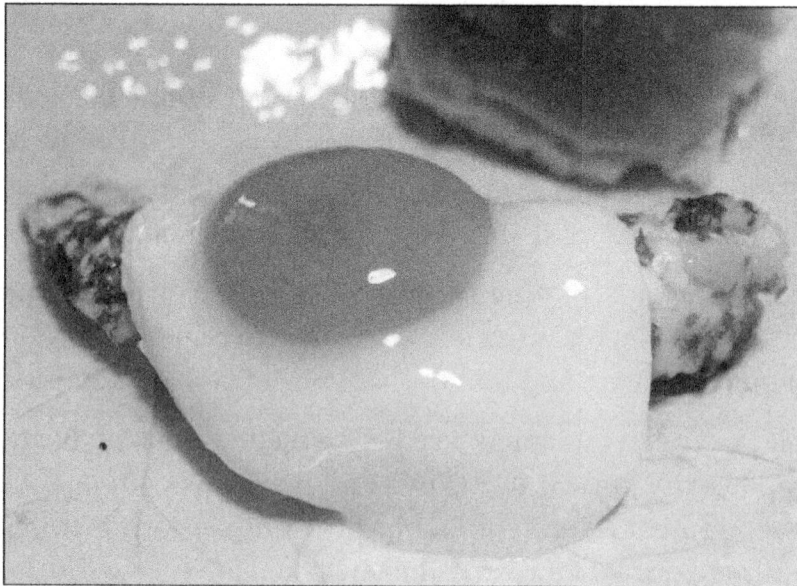

Perfect poaching! Poached egg on a poached gurnard fillet with a fantastically flavoured chervil coat

This is a lot easier and quicker than it might seem!

Begin by putting 8 cm of water into a medium saucepan (for the fish) and 1cm water into a frying pan (for the eggs), then putting them over a medium heat to begin getting them to the boil.

Lay the gurnard fillets on a board, drizzle half a glug of good olive oil over each one and rub it over as evenly as possible. Scrunch a pinch of sea salt over each and sprinkle half the chervil over each fillet as evenly as you can.

Chervil is a lovely herb, great with fish, and easy to grow, all year round

Place one of the fillets gently on the palm of your hand and carefully slide it into the open poaching bag on the right hand side. Don't worry about the pieces of chervil that are bound to fall off! Repeat with the other fillet, sliding it in to the left hand side next to the first. Pick up fallen chervil with pallet knife, hold over gurnard, and shake off.

Now tie the bag loosely, press down on the bag with one hand to squeeze out as much air as possible before tightening the knot with the other hand. Then double knot the bag, keeping it flat at all times.

87

When the two pans of water are boiling turn the frying pan to low so that it is at a simmer and shake in 4 shakes of vinegar. Now gently, holding the poaching bag so it is as flat as possible, place it in the medium sized pan.

When the fish poach water has returned to the boil, it won't take long to cook. Crack an egg and break it as low as possible over the frying pan, then repeat with the second egg.

Cooking time for the fish will be 6 minutes, by which time the eggs will be ready, with the whites set and yolks still yellow and runny. Turn off the heat under both pans.

Lift the poached gurnard bag out of the pan, fingers should be fine, using the knot sealing the bag to hold it, place it on a plate. Ensure the knot is to the top of the bag and snip off the knot using the scissors. *There will be very hot liquor inside the bag so be careful now!* Hold down one side of the bag and use the spatula or pallet knife, sliding it underneath one of the poached fillets, to lift it out and once over the serving plate slide it gently off and onto the plate. Repeat with the other fillet.

To remove the poached eggs, gently use a knife to separate them, and a plastic spatula or egg slice to lift them out one at a time, shaking them a little to remove excess water, before sliding them gently onto the gurnard.

I like mine with toast, but a soft roll is also great for mopping up the runny egg yolk that always escapes and those wonderful juices!

Told you this was easier than it sounds!!

Turbot cakes with chilli ▲

turbot, cooked, cold, around two good handfuls

new potatoes, smallish, 12, cooked and squished

chilli, red or green, fresh, 1, chopped, with seeds if you like it hot

egg, 1, beaten

goats' butter, 1 good knob

vegetable oil, 1 glug

portions, 2 (6 cakes)

OK, so you probably wouldn't buy turbot specifically for cakes, but what a great breakfast to follow a turbot dinner for two.

Simply flake the cold turbot and put into a mixing bowl with the potato and chopped chilli. Add the egg and mix together well.

There will be enough mix for around 6 cakes, maybe a couple more. Using your hands scoop out the mixture and shape into patties around 7.5 cm across and 1.9 cm deep and put on one side.

Heat the oil in a frying pan over a medium light and when warm add the butter. When the butter has melted simply add the cakes, carefully as they will be a bit fragile, letting them turn golden brown before turning – allow three minutes. Turn them carefully and cook for two more minutes and you've got your breakfast. Easy.

Meat & Poultry

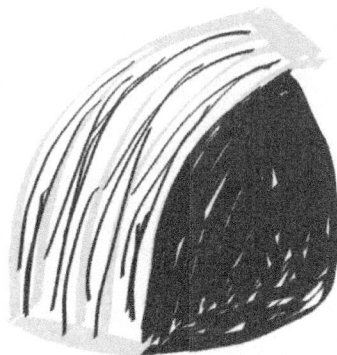

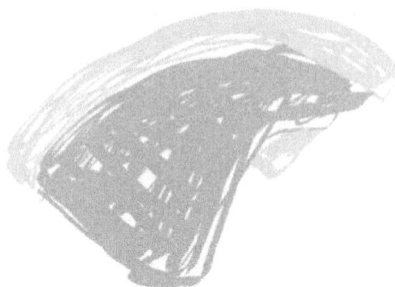

Awesome avocado and chicken hash ▲

avocados, 2 peeled and roughly chopped

onion, 1 medium, or 2 banana shallots, peeled, finely chopped

cooked chicken, 2 handfuls, shredded

ripe tomatoes, 3 medium, chopped

goats' butter, good knob

chilli red or green, mild, 1 small finely chopped without seeds (optional)

chicken stock, 250ml reduced from 500 ml

salt to taste

ground black pepper, be generous!

2 portions

Sweat the onion and chilli in the oil and butter until soft.

Add the chicken and tomatoes and stir for 5 minutes. Add the reduced chicken stock and simmer for 10 minutes. Add the avocado and stir for a further 10 minutes until starting to melt.

Delicious with fresh crusty bread, bruschetta or gluten-free crackers (see page 147).

Also great with duck.

Beef, stir-fried with mushrooms and bean sprouts ▲

beef, sirloin steaks, 500 gm, fat trimmed off, thinly sliced

ginger, fresh, 75cm, thumb base thickness, thinly sliced

toasted sesame oil, 2 glugs

rice wine vinegar, 2 glugs

water, 2 teaspoons

Tamari soy sauce, 2 glugs

salt, 2 good pinches

cornflour, 2 teaspoons

water, 2 tablespoons

mushrooms, chestnut, 10, medium button, thinly sliced

more toasted sesame oil, 2 glugs

bean sprouts, ½ a packet, soaked in salted water for 1 hour

2 portions

Put all the ingredients as far down as the salt (including it) into a bowl and mix well. Cling and put in the fridge for 30 minutes then remove. Put a wok over a hot heat and when hot add the marinated beef mixture and stir-fry for just one minute – the beef should still be slightly pink when you remove the wok from the heat. Turn into a bowl and set aside.

Tip the cornflour into a mug, add water, stir briskly until you have a paste.

Reheat the wok and when hot add the sesame oil. As it begins to bubble, add the mushrooms and bean sprouts and stir-fry for 3 – 4 minutes, then add the beef mixture.

Remove from the heat, stir in the thickening and put back over the heat, turned down to medium. Keep stirring as the mixture thickens and the beef heats up. By the time it is all nicely simmering, the liquor will have thickened and you're good to go. Serve and enjoy!

Cadan's Christmas chicken sausages ▲

chicken, uncooked, no skin, 500gm finely chopped

gluten-free breadcrumbs, 90 gm

mace, 1 tbspn, heaped

salt, ¼ tspn

white pepper, ¼ tspn

lemon, 1, zest only, finely chopped

parsley, fresh, 1 handful, finely chopped

sage, 15 medium to large leaves, central veins removed, chopped

water, 28 ml

Portions: This will make 9 to 12 sausages depending on how large you make them!

Surprisingly these sausages hold together very well despite the fact they have no skin. They are more fragile than sausages with skins so handle them carefully when moving them into the pan and turning them; using a plastic spatula or pallet knife for turning them will reduce the chances of them breaking while cooking.

I use a fresh whole chicken, and find I get around 500 grams of unskinned meat from half a breast and one boned thigh and leg. It's easier to use the breast meat as it doesn't need deboning though and you can save the thighs and legs (and wings) for cooking a meal of my Southern Fried Chicken (page 93) for which they are perfect!

If you end up with slightly more or less meat simply adjust the quantities of the other ingredients accordingly.

Note: Cadan is my partner's younger brother who has many food intolerances. He adores sausages, but so many contain gluten I make these and the Lincolnshire ones (page 121) for him and everybody loves them!

Sumptuous freshly rolled sausages ready for the pan

Add the chicken, then breadcrumbs and remaining dry ingredients to a large bowl and using your fingers mix together well. Then add the water and mix in, continuing to mix until the water is well absorbed and the consistency is firm but malleable, similar to that of sausage meat.

Allow to rest for 30 minutes on the kitchen counter for the flavours to meld and the breadcrumbs to continue to take up the moisture.

You just need a flat surface to roll the sausages so I use a large glass chopping board, but a plastic board or the work surface itself work well. I don't use wood as it tends to be warmer which can hamper the rolling.

Simply take out what you guess is enough mix for one sausage, place it on the board and pat it using both hands into a long oval shape. Then using the fingers of both hands together, roll it back and forth, tapping the ends with your fingers occasionally to make them vertical.

The sausage will firm up, reduce in diameter and increase in length quite quickly and you will soon have your first sausage! Carry on rolling until it is around 2 cm in diameter and if it looks a little long simply cut it to the length you'd like.

Pat the ends of the sausage to make them vertical again. Make the ends as near as possible the same diameter as the rest of the sausage and then lift it carefully onto a plate. If the sausage is too short simply take a little more mixture from the bowl for the next one. Carry on until the mix is all used.

These sausages freeze well. To freeze them simply lay them carefully side by side in a small freezer bag, leaving air in the bag before tying it to create space around the sausages before putting the bag in the freezer. Don't make layers of sausages for the freezer as they may join together before freezing, making it difficult to separate them when they defrost. Rather, use two bags rather than one.

Heat a non-stick frying pan with a table spoon of vegetable oil over a low to medium heat and gently place the sausages in the pan. Cook the sausages for around fifteen minutes, turning them three or four times so they are cooked on each side.

While needing to make sure they are cooked right through you don't want to overcook them and although the cooking is over a low heat, the heat will work right through the sausages ensuring they are properly cooked while remaining succulent and juicy. Try a taster after fifteen minutes and if you'd like them cooked more thoroughly, just leave them longer and taste again after another five minutes.

For a special treat you could try these lovely sausages in crispy butter pastry as Christmas sausage rolls:

Cadan's Christmas chicken sausage rolls

For 10 sausage rolls make around 485 gm of crispy butter pastry using the recipe and quantities on pg 93, wrap it in cling and leave in the fridge for 30 minutes. Take from the fridge and leave it for 5 minutes before rolling.

Flour a piece of baking parchment thoroughly, rub flour over the rolling pin and coat your hands well with flour. Roll your pastry ball around the counter to coat it thoroughly and re-flour the parchment. Turn on the oven to bring up to 190°C / 170°C fan.

Press your dough down, on the centre of the parchment to a thickness of around 4cm to 5 cm, then form into a rectangle twice as long on one side as the other, by using the palms of your hands tapping the edges of the dough and re-flatten before rolling out into a rectangle. Re-flour the pastry and rolling pin often during the rolling.

Line up your sausages on the pastry in two rows of 5, side by side around 6cm apart, with the rows almost but not quite butting up against each other. Use a knife to cut the pastry between the rows, then trim the outer edges of the pastry with a knife so that the pastry is in line with the ends of the sausages.

Now cut between the individual sausages so each is now sitting on its own individual pastry square, its coat.

Now to assemble the first sausage roll, slide a pallet knife underneath one side of one of the coats and out the other side to loosen it, then use the pallet knife to gently lift the edge of the coat up and over towards the middle of the sausage. Repeat with the other side of the coat and use your fingers to gently tap the two sides of the coat together.

Now repeat with each sausage and coat until they're all assembled. Beat an egg and brush the egg mix gently over the sausage rolls then lift up the parchment gently, place it on a baking tray and place into the oven for 35-40 minutes. Take a look after 35 minutes and they should be a golden brown, if they're not quite there, they'll be cooked but to develop the colour just put them back for 5 or so minutes.

Remove from the oven, and lift the sausage rolls from the baking tray carefully onto a cooling rack. Use a fish-slice because they will be hot and coated underneath in melted butter!

Just give them a few minutes to cool slightly and enjoy!

Pink stew, with chicken and beetroot ▲

chicken, ½, with skin, jointed, trimmed and chopped into bite sized pieces, bones in

beetroot, medium / large, 2, peeled, sliced, trimmed into bite sized pieces

onions, large, 2, peeled, chopped

garlic, 4 cloves, peeled, chopped

potato, medium / large, peeled, diced into small cubes, ½cm

chicken stock, made with beetroot not carrot (pg 13), 1½ litres

parsley, including stalks, chopped, 1 handful

fresh bay, 3 leaves

spinach, tough stalks removed, 3 good handfuls

salt, 3 good pinches

ground black pepper, 1 tspn, more if you like it peppery, taste at the end

white wine vinegar, 1 ½ tbspn

vegetable oil, 1 glug

Portions,4

First heat a large saucepan over a medium heat and when hot add the oil, then the onions and garlic. fry stirring occasionally until they are soft and translucent, around 5 minutes.

Add the chicken pieces and bay leaves and fry for 10 minutes, stirring every couple of minutes.

Now add the beetroot and potato and fry for three minutes, then add the stock and parsley. Turn up the heat to bring to the boil, then reduce the heat until the stew is simmering nicely, partially cover with a lid.

Stir every 10 minutes, using a wooden spatula to drag along the bottom of the pan, moving the 'melting' potato into the body of the stew otherwise it will stick and burn. Keep simmering and stirring for 1 hour.

Now add the spinach and vinegar, and salt and pepper, and simmer for 10 more minutes after which your intriguingly colourful stew will be ready!

Ladle into dishes and add a spoonful or two of goat's or sheep's yoghurt if you like.

Gurnard's Head. The arch once led to a copper mine.

Chicken and crab jallops

red pepper, 1, seeded, pithed and chopped

onions, medium, 2 red, 1 white, peeled, chopped

garlic, 4 cloves, peeled, finely chopped

runner or green string beans, topped and tailed, sliced into 2.5cm lengths, 1 good handful

wild garlic, 20 leaves, chopped

jalapeno pepper sliced into 10 rings and chopped, or 1½- 2 peppers sliced if you like it hot

rice, long grain, ¼ litre

crab stock, ¾ litre, boiling

chicken breast, uncooked, 1 large, thinly sliced, trimmed into 2.5cm square pieces

sweet paprika, 1 tspn

lemon or lime leaves, 4

good olive oil

salt, for seasoning, 2 good pinches

Portions, 4

Add the oil to a large saucepan and heat over a medium heat. When hot add the pepper, and garlic, and fry for 5 minutes.

Then add the beans and paprika, stir in, turn the heat down and fry for a further 15 minutes.

Add the rice and the salt, stir in and fry for 1 – 2 minutes

Now add the boiling stock and lemon or lime leaves and simmer for 10 minutes.

Sprinkle the chicken pieces over the surface, use a fork or spoon to push the chicken pieces below the surface and into the rice DON'T stir. Simmer for a further 10 minutes by which time the rice will have expanded and become light and fluffy.

Finally sprinkle the jalapeno and wild garlic over, turn off the heat but leave the pan where it is for 5 minutes.

You're there! Just spoon your lovely chicken crab rice dish onto your plates and enjoy.

Sunrise at high tide near the quay at Gorran Haven

Chicken drumsticks, BBQd ▲

drumsticks, free range as they have plumper thighs, as many as needed

large fresh lemons, ½ per drumstick

salt

important – use a cool or cooling BBQ, not a hot one, ideally with a rack that can be lowered as the coals get cooler

2 drumsticks, especially plump ones, makes an ideal portion

People often barbeque drumsticks over a high heat and end up with them being cooked or overcooked on the outside and undercooked on the inside. By cooking them for a long time over cooling coals, for around 1 hour, they lose much less moisture, maintain a lot more taste, and cook through well.

Cooked this way the drumsticks are also delicious cold, so are ideal to cook as the last part of a BBQ session, because they'll be ready about an hour after the previous course was finished, so people may be ready for more, and if not, they are fantastic cold!

When the coals are cooling, put the drumsticks on the BBQ grill, not too near the coals, with the grill on the top level. The idea is to heat the inside of the drumsticks slowly until they are cooking in their own juices, but without breaking the skin with the heat, to keep as much of the juices as possible on the inside! They will take 45 – 60 minutes to cook and are a perfect way to make the most of your coals.

When the skin nearest the coals has browned, turn 180 degrees, then immediately squeeze the fresh lemon over, which cools down the skin, and sprinkle some salt over.

When the skin has browned underneath, again turn 180 degrees, give another squeeze of lemon, and some more salt, then turn back 90 degrees to be cooking on one of the uncooked sides. Repeat the turning process after around 10 minutes, again squeezing lemon and adding salt.

Carry on for around 1 hour, turning 90 degrees every 10 minutes, with a squeeze of lemon each time, gradually lowering the grill as the coals get cooler, or until the skin is just beginning to break, let them rest for a few minutes, and you'll have absolutely fantastic chicken drumsticks that will be irresistible – even to those who say they're full!

Dodman Point in the background. Lambs by the SW coast path not thinking about barbeques!

Chicken leek and mushroom pie

chicken, 200g - 250g, cooked, bite sized pieces left over from roast, or from roasted breasts

leek, 1, large, cut in matchstick style

mushrooms, 12, button, chestnut, cut in half

chicken gravy, thick, 200ml, or reduced and thickened chicken stock (page 13)

crispy butter pastry, see page 152

goats' butter, 6 small knobs

egg, 1, beaten

2 – 4 portions depending on how hungry you are

This dish is really easy to make and a great way to finish off the chicken after a Sunday roast. First preheat the oven to 180ºC, 160°C fan.

Simply place the chicken in your pie dish around a pie bird, sprinkle the leeks on top of the chicken then spread the mushrooms on top of the leeks. Now pour the gravy over the mushrooms making the coating as even as possible, and swish the mushrooms around until they are all coated.

Now simply place 5 knobs of butter evenly spread around the mushrooms, using the sixth to wipe around the top edge of the dish itself, then place the pastry over and crimp the edges, not too hard, pierce the pastry in the centre above the pie bird and brush the pie with the egg. If you don't have a pie bird just pierce 2 short holes around 12mm long in the centre of the pastry. This is to let steam out as the pie cooks so it doesn't boil over.

Place on the middle shelf of the oven and leave for around 50 minutes when the pie lid should be a beautiful golden brown.

Chilli con pollo ▲

chicken breast, 425 grams, small diced

orange pepper, 2 roasted, skinned & chopped

butternut squash, ½, peeled, deseeded, diced, drizzled with oil, roasted
(30 minutes, 180°C, 160°C fan) or try with sweet potato for a change

cannellini beans, 400 gram tin, drained

tomatoes, chopped, 400 gram tin

onion, 1, large, or 2 medium, chopped

chillis, red, 3 or 4, to taste, small, chopped, seeds in

cumin, ground, 2 tablespoons

coriander, ground, 1 tablespoon

water, 1 cupful

vegetable oil, 1 glug

salt, to taste

4 portions

This is a lovely dish, a little like chilli con carne, but creamier and lighter.

First fry the onion gently until soft and translucent, around 5 minutes then
add the chicken pieces, stirring until they have lost their pinkness. Now
add all the other ingredients except the beans, stir and bring to a simmer,
partially cover the pan with a lid and simmer for 45 minutes. Stir every 15
minutes and add more water if the chilli looks a little dry. Try adding ¾ of
the chillis now, and more if you like after tasting around 30 minutes later.

Now add the beans and stir well, bring back to a simmer and cook for
another further 45 minutes, continuing to stir every 15 minutes and adding
more water if necessary. Keeping the lid partially over the pan should
prevent the liquid steaming off, and allow the moist melding of the spices
with the chicken and beans, giving great tastes and textures.

Cornish pasty, with crispy butter pastry

Don't be put off by the length of this recipe! This is really simple stuff but the technique or method needs explanation because you're working with gluten-free pastry. Trust me, I know this from experience!

beef skirt, 180 gm, skin/membrane removed, sliced, 1cm cubed

onion, medium, ½ ish (80 gm, peeled, chopped

potato, peeled, 155 gm, diced, 1cm cubed

swede, peeled, 155gm, 1cm diced

salt, 4 – 6 good pinches

white pepper, ½ tspn

egg, 1, beaten

Crispy butter pastry dough, 2 pasties worth, around 485 gm, see the recipe on page 152

These quantities will make 2 pasties.

Make the pastry first following the recipe on page 152, and while it is resting in the fridge for half an hour prepare the pasty filling as described above. Place the meat and chopped onion onto a plate and mix them together, then sprinkle a good pinch of salt over and mix together well, then split into two portions on the plate.

Now place the diced potatoes on a large plate, sprinkle with a pinch of salt, mix the salt with the potato and split into 2 portions. Place the diced swede onto the same plate, to the side of the potato, sprinkle with a pinch of salt. Mix the swede and salt together and split into two portions.

Now turn on the oven and preheat to 190°C, 170°C fan.

The rolling of the pastry and forming into pasties is, as those of you who have made gluten-free pastry before will know, not as straight forward as making pastry, pasties and pies using flour containing gluten. That's because gluten-free flour doesn't contain the "glue" that keeps most pastry together, helps it to stretch and makes it easier to work and fold.

So, for those of you that haven't made and worked with gluten-free dough before this could be a bit of an adventure!

After removing the dough from the fridge and leaving it to warm for 5 minutes, split it into two. Form each half into a ball by rolling softly between the palms of your hands. Take one of the balls and roll it around a well-floured piece of baking parchment 32 cm square, then re-flour the WHOLE of the rest of the parchment.

Now press down on the ball with the palm of one hand until it is around 3 - 4 cm thick. Sprinkle more flour over the dough, rub flour over the rolling pin, and sprinkle plenty more flour every two passes of the roller, rolling out to around 26 cm diameter circles. Don't worry if your finished circle is a bit ovally!

If the pastry ends up over the edge of the parchment use the pallet knife to trim it back until the pastry edge is 1 cm, ¼ in, inside the parchment. Set the cuttings aside, keeping them flat, until the pasty is assembled as you might need it for patching, which would be normal. No cuttings? Don't worry, you'll have some if you need them once you've folded over your pasty top! Begin assembling the filling using this picture as a guide.

Pasty filling in lines, of meat and onions, potato, and swede

First, take one of the portions of meat and onions and place it in a quarter moon shape on the left of your pasty, around 2½ cm from the edge of the circle. Now take one portion of potato and spread it in a line next to the meat, and then take a portion of swede and place it in a line next to the potato. The right side of the swede should be just short of the halfway point of your circle.

Use a pastry brush to lightly brush the flour away from the edges of your circle and off the parchment, avoiding disturbing it's edges. Finish the filling by sprinkling it with half the white pepper as evenly as you can.

To begin the folding over of the pasty top, gently raise the parchment underneath the unfilled half with your left hand so that you can slide your right hand, palm side up, underneath until the pastry is firmly resting on the palm of your hand, with the edge of your right hand firmly butting up against the line of swede. Remove your left hand from the parchment. Now, smoothly and fairly swiftly, flip your right hand over and leftwards taking the parchment and pastry with it so that they fold over the filling with the unfilled edge sitting as closely as possible over the filled edge. If the fit isn't exact don't worry.

Gently peel back the parchment and lay it flat. Trim round the pastry edges and use the trimmings to patch any holes revealed when the parchment was pulled back, gently tapping them into place. Don't try to crimp the top and bottom edges together, just press them together gently. They will seal well during cooking.

Now carefully, holding the left and right edges of the parchment, lift it with the pasty onto your baking tray and simply cut off with scissors the half not containing the pasty.

Now repeat with the second pasty and finally trim any parchment overhanging the baking tray with scissors to prevent it burning, brush the pasties with the beaten egg and lift your tray into the preheated oven.

The aroma of cooking pasty is fantastic, and will be a real pleasure as it builds over the next three quarters of an hour or so!

Take a peek at your pasties after 45 minutes by which time they should be a lovely golden brown. By now the filling will be cooked so you're cooking for a deeper colour if you leave them longer. They might need another 5 minutes.

Delicious Cornish pasties with crispy butter pastry fresh from the oven

Double chick ratatouille

chick 1: cooked chicken, 2 large handfuls

chick 2: cooked chick peas, 1 ladleful

onions, 2 medium, chopped

garlic, 2 cloves, finely chopped

red pepper, 1, chopped

courgette, 1, chopped

chopped tomatoes, ½ tin

chicken stock, 250 ml, (see my recipe on page 13)

17 black olives

olive oil, 1 glug

salt and black pepper to taste

4 portions

Sweat the onion, garlic, red pepper and courgette in the oil for 15 minutes. Add the chopped tomatoes, and chicken stock and cook for further 15 minutes. Add the chicken, chick peas and black olives and cook for further 20 minutes. Season to taste.

Variations: substitute turkey, guinea fowl, duck or pheasant for the chicken.

Duck in lemon chilli sauce with pasta

cooked duck meat, 3-4 good handfuls, small bite sized pieces

smoked streaky bacon, 50 g small chopped

lemon, small, zest chopped + juice

duck stock, reduced, 750 ml

garlic, 2 cloves, peeled, and squashed flat

chillis, red, 4 tiny hot guys, whole (don't break up during cooking !)

shallots, or small onions, 3, finely chopped

thyme, 4 - 5 good sprigs, whole

white or red wine vinegar, 100 ml

flour, plain, 2 tablespoons

olive or rapeseed oil, 1 tablespoon

salt and pepper seasoning, to taste

pasta of choice, enough for 2

Parmesan or pecorino cheese, grated, to taste

portions 2

Heat a large saucepan over medium heat, when hot add the oil, then bacon and fry until fat is running. Add the shallot or onions, and continue to fry, stirring frequently to stop it all sticking. When all golden (after 10 - 15mins), add ½ handful of duck, stirring frequently for 5 minutes. Then add lemon juice and zest, garlic, chillies, and thyme and stir in.

Stir for a couple of minutes then add the flour and mix, stir for 3 – 4 minutes. Then add the vinegar, stirring in gently (don't want to split the chillies), and fry for around 3 minutes, stirring occasionally, or until mixture is beginning to look a bit dry (the vinegar has bubbled away), then add the duck stock and the rest of the duck.

Stir in. Add salt and pepper to taste. You will now have a sauce which will gradually thicken, so cover and stir occasionally (carefully - you still don't want to split the chillies), simmering for 30 minutes.

The pasta should take around 8 - 12 minutes depending on the type and how al dente you like it - simply time it so it is ready for when the sauce is cooked at the 30 minute stage.

Now drain the pasta and add to your bowls, spoon the sauce over and add cheese to taste.

Take care with the chillies - only break them open and eat if you like it hot, otherwise leave!

Sea thrift. Mevagissey lighthouse in the background.

Fabulously flexible frittata ▲

sweet potato, 320 gm peeled, medium diced (1 – 1.5cm cubes)

cherry tomatoes, 14, ideally different colours

spinach, 150 gm, non-tough stalks included, large pieces

courgette, 200 gm

goats' soft cheese log, 125 gm, broken into small pieces

onion, 1, large, peeled, chopped

eggs, 5

oat milk, 2 tbspns

sweet paprika, 2 teaspoons

garlic, 3 cloves, peeled and chopped

bay leaves, 5

sage, 10 medium leaves, central vein removed, chopped (plus ½ handful thyme if you like)

good olive oil, 4 glugs

ground black pepper, 27 twists

salt, 2 x ½ teaspoon

portions, 4

Note: This is made using a 20 cm diameter (across the base) frying pan and a piece of kitchen foil cut to size to act as an upwardly mobile lid as the frittata rises! It is cooked in one pan over a single gas or electric ring and is very camping friendly.

Instead of cheese and tomato, try it using 3 or 4 sausages or a couple of handfuls of shelled king prawns to check out the flexibility.

Experiment away!

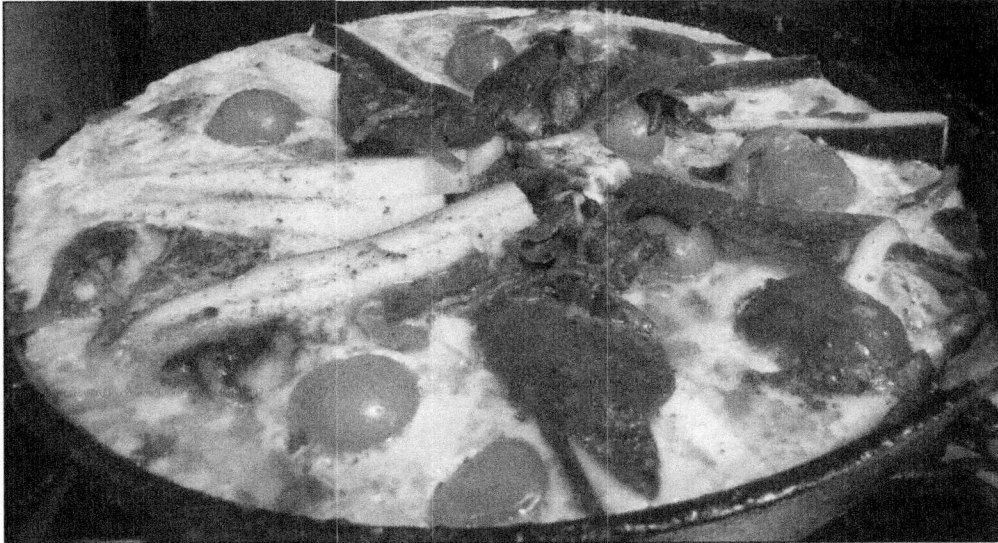

Delicious goats' cheese frittata with sliced courgette, orange, red, and sunburst tomatoes and spinach

Heat the pan over a medium heat then add 1 glug of olive oil, then the sweet potato. Fry for 10 minutes, stir and turn 4 times until lovely and golden brown on most sides.

Sprinkle a glug of olive oil over, stir, then add onion, garlic, bay, sage, thyme, stir well. Add the paprika, black pepper, and 1 x ½ teaspoon of salt, stir and turn and fry for 10 minutes stirring and turning 3 more times.

Cut the courgette in half and slice one half into chunky slices, and the other half into triangular strips to decorate the top of the dish; you can do this by cutting the half into half along its length, then each of the halves into half along their lengths and then each quarter into half along their lengths.

Break the eggs into a large glass bowl, add the second ½ tsp of salt and the oat milk and beat with a balloon whisk for 1 minute.

Add a glug of olive oil then the spinach to the pan, turning everything over using a fork to mix the spinach leaves in as far as possible. Many will remain on the surface but quite a few will stir into the mix as the leaves soon wilt.

Now add the courgette slices, tomatoes, and cheese pieces and do your best using your fingers carefully and a fork to work them towards the bottom of the mix. Some just will not play and remain on or near the surface. Don't worry too much as their colour will add a marvellous visual flourish to the dish when cooked.

Add a final glug of olive oil, give everything a quick stir, pushing those awkward tomatoes and courgette pieces, and the resurfaced spinach leaves and cheese down as much as possible, before using the balloon whisk on the egg mix again and then pour the mix over the colourful contents of the pan. Use your fingers to spread everything as evenly as possible and place the triangular courgette strips in a star pattern on top.

Turn the heat down to very low then place the kitchen foil over and fold it down the sides of the frying pan making the fit as tight as possible by putting slight twists in it. The objective here is to let as little heat as possible to escape from gaps around the foil.

The frittata will take around 35 to 40 minutes to cook depending how low you've been able to turn your heat. The longer the better so the lower the better. After 20 – 30 minutes the foil may well begin to magically rise which is great, but don't worry if it doesn't. How much the frittata rises and when will depend on how many of the ingredients remain on the surface and how many have remained near the base.

After 35 minutes lift the foil cover and test by gently stabbing the frittata with a knife blade. If it remains largely dry when removed your dish is cooked. If it is still wet, put the lid back and carry on cooking for 5 minutes and test again. Repeat if necessary and if in doubt cut a piece and taste!

Gently slide the tip of a plastic spatula down between the edge of the frittata and the pan to separate it in case of sticking, and repeat right round the pan. Then use a knife to quarter the frittata and an egg slice to gently lift the quarters from the pan and onto plates. Enjoy!

Goose pie with mashed potatoes

roasted goose meat, 300g – 450g, cut into thin slices

celery, 2 sticks, ends removed and chopped into medium sized chunks

carrot, medium, 1, peeled, sliced

onion, large, 1, peeled, thinly sliced

leek, 1, ends removed, sliced

mushrooms, button, 8, sliced

goose stock, 1 litre. (My stock recipe is on page 13), use chicken or duck stock if no goose stock is available or can be made

crispy butter pastry, 1 square, or rolled to cover 400mm pie dish with 50mm of overlap, see recipe on page 152

potatoes, 4 medium, peeled, boiled and plain mashed with butter

groundnut oil, 1 glug

goats' butter, 1 knob

egg, 1, beaten

2 – 4 portions depending on hungry you are!

Take half of the stock and simmer for an hour or so to reduce it to around 250ml and set aside to thicken for the gravy.

Heat a frying pan over a medium heat until hot and add the oil, then add the onions and carrots. Fry gently until the onions are soft and translucent Remove with slotted spoon, put onto kitchen towel to dry.

Now we're ready to assemble the pie. I like to build pies like this in layers so I start with a layer of goose meat on the base, followed by onion and carrot, then leek and celery, then mushrooms. Then repeat until all the ingredients are in. Clear a space in the centre for a pie bird and place it. Preheat oven to 190ºC, 170ºC fan while you're finishing the preparation.

Next, thicken the reduced stock. Reheat it, and while heating, add a teaspoon of cornflour to a cup and mix with a tiny amount of water until it's a very thick paste. Remove the stock from the heat and, stirring constantly, add the thickening liquid then put back over the heat stirring constantly. The gravy will thicken after a minute or two. Pour it evenly over the top of the pie filling. Use a fork to gently move the ingredients around slightly to allow the gravy to soak through and coat them all.

Take the knob of butter and rub it around the rim of the pie dish then gently lay the pastry over and press down with a fork - not too hard as the lid will shrink while cooking (which is why you need the overlap) and you don't want it to split. Use a fork or pointed knife to make a hole over the pie bird, and brush pastry with beaten egg. If you don't have a pie bird cut two short slits, 12mm in the centre of the lid for the steam to escape.

The oven should be up to temperature by now, so place dish on middle shelf and cook until the pastry is a lovely golden brown, which should be around 40 minutes. A little longer or shorter won't matter. If you're worried about overflows place on a baking tray.

When the pie is finished take it from the oven and reheat the mash in the microwave (2 minutes on high), or if already hot, serve onto the plates. Gently remove the lid from the pie and set aside, then spoon out pie portions onto the plates.

Now, carefully, cut the lid into shapes and sizes that will cover the pie portions and place over, then replace what is left of the lid (if any!), and you're ready to take your delicious dish to the table.

Guinea Fowl pie

guinea fowl stock, 500ml, see page 13.

roasted guinea fowl meat, 150g – 200g, trimmed into bite sized pieces

onion, medium, 1, chopped, fried in ground nut oil, until soft, well drained

mushrooms, button, 10, sliced

carrot, 1, medium, peeled and sliced

crispy butter pastry rolled to cover a 200mm diameter pie dish with a 50mm overlap, see recipe on page 152. Freeze the dough not used.

butter, 2 knobs

cornflour, 1 teaspoon

water, 3 teaspoons

egg, 1 beaten

2 – 4 portions, depending how hungry you are.

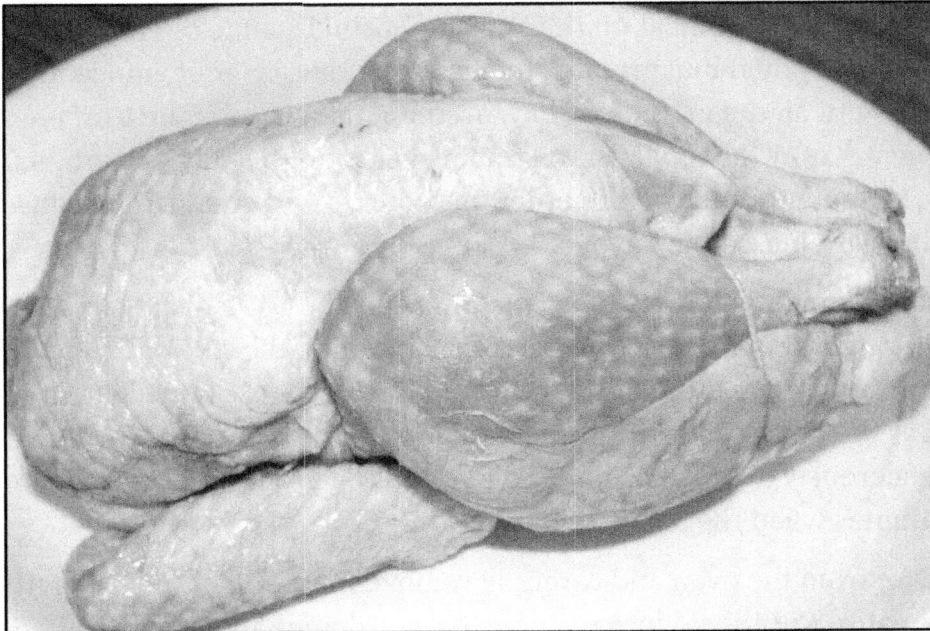

A succulent guinea fowl ready for the oven

Guinea Fowl pie is great on its own, but especially great with mash to mop up the gravy.

If you've got guinea fowl meat for the pie the chances are you've also got a carcass to make the stock with – if not, use chicken stock instead.

A good 2 - 4 portion pie dish is 200mm diameter and 75mm high, and is just right for this dish.

Turn the oven on to preheat to 190ºC, 170ºc fan, then reduce the stock to just 4 tablespoons. Do this gently, simmering rather than brusquely boiling, stirring occasionally. Then add one knob of butter and stir in. Sprinkle the cornflour into a bowl or mug followed by the water and stir into a thick paste. Remove the reduced stock from the heat and add the cornflour paste, stirring continuously. Put back on the heat still stirring continuously until the stock has thickened even more. After a couple of minutes remove from the heat and set aside to go cold.

You'll end up with a semi-solid jelly which is full of flavour and which will become a fantastically flavoured gravy in your pie.

Now assemble the pie, beginning with the pie bird in the middle and a layer of guinea fowl meat on the bottom. Sprinkle some onion over, layer some carrots, then mushrooms, then add another layer of guinea fowl. Repeat until all the ingredients are used up, then use a knife to spread the jelly gently over the top layer. As the pie heats up the jelly will gradually melt, running through all the other ingredients and giving them a luscious coating with incredible flavour.

Use the remaining butter to rub the top edge of the pie dish before laying the pastry over, with plenty of pastry overlapping the side of the dish. Use your fingers to press the pastry down on the top edge of the dish, not too hard as the pastry will shrink and you don't want it to split. Now brush the egg generously over the pastry and place in the preheated oven for around 45 minutes when the pastry will be a lovely golden brown.

Remove from the oven and carefully remove the pie lid, then spoon the pie onto plates. Cut the lid into the appropriate shapes and number of portions, place over the pie portions and serve.

Jolly ginger leek and chicken pie

crispy butter pastry, ½ batch (see page 152)

ginger. large thumb, unpeeled, short matchsticks

onion, 1 large, chopped

leek, 1 large, sliced in rounds

cooked chicken, 3 large handfuls. roughly chopped

chicken stock, 1/2 litre, warmed

goats' butter, 1 knob

plain flour, 2 dspns

flavourless oil, dash

salt and pepper to taste

beaten egg to glaze the pastry

4 portions

Preheat oven to 200ºC 180ºC fan

Melt the butter in a pan, add the plain flour, stir to make a roux. Then stir in the warm chicken stock to make a velouté. Season with salt and pepper.

Sweat the ginger, onion and leek in butter with a dash of oil for 15 minutes then stir in the chicken and the velouté. Place a pie bird in the centre of a 200mm diameter baking dish then pour the pie mix into the dish. If you don't have a pie bird just cut a slit in the pastry after it's placed on top. Rub the top edge of the dish with butter to stop the pastry sticking.

Top the dish with the pastry, leaving a 50mm overhang and brush with beaten egg. Cut a hole directly above the pie bird, or a slit 50 mm long in the middle of the top for steam to escape if you don't have a bird.

Try this pie with turkey, guinea fowl, duck or pheasant if you like - they all go really well with ginger and leek. They're all delicious!!

Lamb - kebabs, Eastern style, marinated, BBQd, with dipping sauce ▲

lamb steaks, 2, cut into bite sized pieces

garlic, 2 cloves, peeled and crushed

curry masala, 2 teaspoons

toasted sesame oil, ½ glug

groundnut oil, ½ glug

white wine, 1 glass

red chilli, 1, small, seeds removed, chopped

goats' butter, 1 knob

crème fraîche or oat cream, 1 big tablespoon

2 portions

First, the heat debate – if you like hot then leave the seeds in the chilli.

Now make the marinade, which will later become the dipping sauce, by adding the garlic, curry masala, oils, wine and chilli to a bowl. Then simply put the lamb in the bowl and stir, making sure that all of the lamb pieces have been coated. Cover and set aside for 2 hours. Take the lamb from the bowl and put on skewers, ready to put on the grill.

Now, reduce the marinade by putting it into a saucepan and either putting it onto the barbeque grill or a medium light on the hob, and simmer to reduce gradually, adding the butter and crème fraîche or oat cream, which will give a nice sheen to the sauce. Reduce until it is around ½ the original volume, taking 15 to 30 minutes depending on how much it is bubbling, and allow to cool.

Now just barbeque the lamb skewers - around 6 to 8 minutes - quite close to the coals, turning frequently. This goes very well with barbequed aubergine, with the dipping sauce drizzled or spread over them as well as being used to dunk the lamb.

Lincolnshire sausages ▲

pork, minced, 500 gm

gluten-free breadcrumbs, 90 gm

mace, 1 tbspn

salt, ¼ tspn

ground white pepper, ¼ tspn

ground black pepper, ½ tspn

sage, 15 medium to large leaves, central veins removed, chopped

water, 28 ml

portions: This will make 9 to 12 sausages depending on how large you make them!

Lovely Linkies sizzling in the pan

Surprisingly these sausages hold together very well despite the fact they have no skin. They are more fragile than sausages with skins though so handle them carefully when moving them into the pan and turning them; using a plastic spatula or pallet knife for turning them will reduce the chances of them breaking while cooking.

Add the pork, then breadcrumbs followed by the remaining dry ingredients to a large bowl and using your fingers mix together well. Then add the water and mix in, continuing to mix until the water is well absorbed and the consistency is firm but malleable, similar to that of sausage meat.

Allow to rest for 30 minutes on the kitchen counter for the flavours to meld and the breadcrumbs to continue to take up the moisture.

You just need a flat surface to roll the sausages so I use a large glass chopping board, but a plastic board or the work surface itself will work well. I don't use wood as it tends to be warmer which can hamper the rolling process.

Simply take out what you guess is enough sausage mix for one sausage, a small handful, place it on the board and pat it using both hands into an oval shape then tap the ends to make them vertical. Then, using the fingers of both hands together, roll it back and forth, tapping the ends occasionally with your fingers to bring them back to vertical.

The sausage will firm up, reduce in diameter and increase in length quite quickly and you will soon have your first sausage! Carry on rolling until it is around 2 cm in diameter and if it looks a little long simply cut it to the length you'd like. Pat the ends of the sausage to make them vertical again. Make the ends as near as possible the same diameter as the rest of the sausage and then place it carefully on a plate. If the sausage is too short simply take a little more mixture from the bowl for the next one and carry on until the mix is all used.

These sausages freeze well. To freeze them simply lay them carefully side by side in a small freezer bag, leaving air in the bag before tying it to create space around the sausages before putting the bag in the freezer. Don't make layers of sausages for the freezer as they may join together before freezing making it difficult to separate them when they defrost. Rather, use two bags rather than one.

Heat a non-stick frying pan with a table spoon of vegetable oil over a low to medium heat and gently place the sausages in the pan. Cook the sausages for around ten minutes, turning them three or four times so they are cooked on each side.

While needing to make sure they are cooked right through you don't want to overcook them and although the cooking is over a low heat, the heat will work right through the sausages ensuring they are properly cooked while remaining succulent and juicy. Try a taster after ten minutes and if you'd like them cooked more thoroughly, just leave them longer and taste again after another five minutes.

Pre-sunrise at Mevagissey harbour.

Nonna's chicken & herb agrodolce fandango ▲

This recipe comes from my sister, Lucia, whose mother-in-law lives in Milan. It is a favourite of my nephews because the soaking of the onions sweetens and softens them.

cooked chicken, 4 large handfuls

chicken stock, 5 ladlefuls

onions, 2 large, sliced in rounds

garlic, 2 cloves, finely chopped or wild garlic, 1 small bunch, chopped

leek, 1, sliced in rounds

potato, 1 medium, small diced

thyme, 5 sprigs

white wine vinegar, 2 tbspns

flavourless oil, 1 glug

salt and black pepper to taste

4 portions

Soak the onions for at least 30 minutes - I have left them for 2 hours - squeeze out the water and sweat them in the oil, with the lid on the pan, for 20 minutes.

Add the potato, garlic, thyme and chicken stock and for further 20 minutes, lid on, then mash the potato into the liquor with a fork and cook for a further 20 minutes.

Add the chicken and the leek and cook for further 15 minutes. Add the vinegar and cook for a further 5 minutes. Season to taste.

Just sublime.

Variations: substitute turkey, guinea fowl, duck or pheasant for the chicken.

Pork - steamed cabbage parcels with pork, tomatoes and basil

cabbages, white, mini, 2

pork loin steaks, 2

tomatoes, plum, small, 10

basil, fresh, 12 leaves

onion, ½, peeled, chopped

garlic, 1 clove, crushed

goats' butter, 2 knobs

groundnut oil, 1 glug

string, around 600 mm

2 portions

You're probably looking at the title of the dish and the ingredients and saying WHAAAAT!... ...how on earth can this be good?......exactly what my partner said the day I put this one together but he was amazed, and so will you be.

First hollow out the cabbages, these are the small white ones. You need to start by carefully cutting out the core, in one piece so you end up with a cone, which you're going to use to seal the cabbage once it has been stuffed.

When you've got the cone out, use a knife or teaspoon to hollow out the cabbage, leaving a thickness of around 15mm of leaves on the outside. Do it carefully to avoid having any holes. Set the cabbage and scoopings aside.

Chop the core, 1/3 of the way down, keep the top 1/3 and discard the bottom 2/3, or eat it raw which I do - I love it.

Remove any fat from the pork and chop it finely. Place a frying pan over a medium heat and when hot, add the oil then the onion and garlic. When the onions are soft and translucent add the pork and fry for a further 3 minutes then remove from the heat, add the butter, and cover the pan. After 2 – 3 minutes stir the mixture then add the tomatoes and basil.

Now spoon the mixture into the cabbages until there is just enough space to replace the top 1/3 of the core which you have saved, insert the core which will act as a plug and seal the pork mix inside the cabbage.

Use half the string on each cabbage to hold the core in place. Wind a piece of string round each cabbage, ensuring it is over the top of the plug, and tying it in place. Do this for each cabbage and you're ready to steam them.

Just place in the steamer, with the scooped out leaves around, and steam for 30 minutes.

A great autumn dish with mashed potato to mop up the delicious juices. Serve after removing the string, with the cabbage the right way up, for the best visual effect.

St Michael's Mount. Animals were once herded there.

Southern fried chicken ▲

chicken breast and leg with thigh, uncooked, 1 of each

plain flour, 100 gm

sweet paprika, 1½ tbspn

salt, 2 good pinches

oat milk, 250 ml

lemon, ¼, juice of

black pepper, ground, ½ tspn – 1 tspn depending how peppery you like it

vegetable oil, 2 glugs

portions, 2

Although this lovely chicken is quite quick to prepare and takes only ½ an hour to cook you'll need patience! For the marinading of the chicken, which takes at least 12 hours, and up to 2 days if you can wait that long!

Prepare the chicken by cutting it into the size of piece that you'd like to be eating once it is cooked. At home I like to separate the thigh from the drumstick and then cut the thigh in in two, and to trim a chicken breast into four or five pieces depending on how big it is.

Heat the oat milk over a medium heat until it's very warm then remove it from the heat and add a pinch of salt and the lemon juice. You may see the milk separate, if so that's great, if not, don't worry. If you're using dairy milk it will definitely separate.

Wait for the milk to cool and pour it into a food bag. Now put your chicken pieces into the bag and tie it or seal it well. Rub the chicken through the bag for thirty seconds and put it in the fridge to marinate. Rub the oat milk into the chicken every few hours while marinading which should take a minimum of twelve hours but can be left for two days to tenderise more and further improve the flavour.

When you're ready to cook, mix the flour, paprika, salt and pepper on a plate. Add the oil to a frying pan large enough to take all the chicken pieces, and put over a highish heat. While the oil is heating take the chicken from the bag, piece by piece and shake it before dropping it onto the flour, tossing it and laying it carefully into the pan. Sear the chicken on the high heat for 2 – 3 minutes then turn it and sear the other side, again for just 2 – 3 minutes.

Turn down the heat until it is EXTREMELY low, as low as you can get it, and cook for 15 minutes. Now turn the chicken again and cook for a further 15 minutes.

Your chicken should now be dark golden brown and ready to eat! My favourite accompaniment is cucumber salad.

Peel around 10 cm, 4 in of cucumber, slice it thinly, sprinkle with white wine vinegar and a little ground wite pepper, Enjoy.

Try it as popcorn chicken as a variation – using smaller, bite sized chicken pieces in the marinade, and cook for 5-10 minutes per side over medium heat instead.

Triumphant Turkish beef delight ▲

minced beef, good quality but not low fat, 500gm

onions, 2 medium, chopped

garlic, 2 cloves, finely chopped

chopped tomatoes, good quality tinned

cabbage, Savoy or hispi, 1/2, chopped

tomato puree, 1/3 tube

sweet paprika, 1 tsp

sumac, 1tsp

chilli powder, 1 tsp

flavourless oil, glug

salt and pepper to taste

water, 125 ml

4 large portions

Sweat the onion and garlic in a wide pan with a lid for 10 minutes. Add the minced beef and stir until it loses colour.

Add the spices and seasoning and stir. Add the chopped tomatoes, water and tomato puree and stir. Cook for 40 minutes, partially covered.

Top with the cabbage, cover and cook for a further 40 minutes.

Delicious with mashed or boiled potatoes, pasta or rice.

Turkey and ham terrine layered with roasted red peppers and parsley, with plum and parsley chutney

turkey, roasted, 225gm, shredded

Parma or Serrano ham, 2 packs or 12 slices

roasted ham, 4 slices, or 150 mm x 150 mm if home cooked, fat removed

peppers, red or orange, roasted & blackened

onion, red, ½ fine chopped

plums, 2, stoned, skin removed and chopped

parsley leaves, fresh, chopped, 1 good handful

white wine vinegar, 1 glug

good olive oil, 1 good glug

salt, 2 teaspoons

caster sugar, 2 teaspoons

Portions, 6 - 8

First, let's roast the peppers – put them on a baking tray, brush with olive oil and put them into a preheated oven at 220ºC, 200ºC fan for 30 minutes. The skins should have blackened the skin should remove easily. Put the peppers, carefully, into a freezer bag, or wrap in cling film and leave for 10 minutes. I don't know how it works, but it does, when you remove the peppers from the bag, the skin will now magically peel off easily. Peel them, remove the seeds and pith, chop them, then set aside.

Now take a loaf tin, around 255 mm x 127 mm x 65 mm and drape the Parma or Serrano ham over the sides. Start by placing one edge of the first piece of ham at the centre of the bottom of the loaf tin, then just drape. This should leave sufficient overhang for the ham to be able fold back over the top of the dish when finished. Then repeat right round the tin, double layering when you've gone round once until the ham is used up.

Now you're going to build up the layers of the terrine, but first season the turkey to taste with salt and pepper, then place around ¼ of it in the bottom of the tin spreading it evenly, then add a slice of roast ham, then around ¼ of the peppers, evenly spread, and repeat. The third layer will be the parsley, so sprinkle the leaves (unchopped) onto the peppers, and repeat the layering until all the ingredients are used up and finishing with a little more turkey on top.

Now fold the Parma or Serrano ham over the top layer as tightly as possible and place the terrine into an oven preheated to 150ºC, 130ºC fan leave for 1½ hours and go and take a well-earned glass of wine!

Now the really clever bit - you need to compress the terrine, probably requiring a house search to find the components that will work! You're going to compress the terrine, under a fairly heavy weight, for 4 hours altogether. I use 2 sets of coasters (wrapped in cling film), stacked to reach 50mm above the tin, then I place 2 very heavy cast iron cooking blocks on top. A house brick or 2 will also work well !

Now for the chutney. Caramelise the onions by frying them in some of the oil very gently over a low heat for 20 to 30 minutes after which they will be dark brown, very soft and very sweet. Then add the chopped plums, stir in the caster sugar and white wine vinegar and continue to fry over the low heat for another 15 minutes, stirring occasionally, after which the plums will be mushy. Then mash with the back of a spoon and put in a serving dish to cool.

After 2 hours remove the coasters and weights and carefully pour the liquor from the tin into a small jug. It is a wonderful jus and goes really well with the terrine. Replace the weights. After another 2 hours drain the liquor into the jug again, then turn the terrine out onto a dish.

When you're ready to eat simply carve the terrine into slices and place them on a plate. Pour some jus over and add a dollop of chutney on the side. A bit fiddly, especially the weighting down part, but well worth the effort to find this creative way of using the last of the Christmas turkey.

Vegetable

Asparagus, fantastic flavour, features here in vegetable stuff but also in soups and salads!

Asparagus, griddled, with egg and pecorino ▲

asparagus spears, 12 - 18 depending on size, woody ends snapped off

eggs, 2

pecorino cheese, 50 - 60 gm, grated

good olive oil, 3 glugs, poured into a small bowl or dish

salt, to taste

Portions, 2

First put your griddle pan over quite a high heat to heat up and while it is heating brush the asparagus spears all over with olive oil.

When the pan is hot lift the asparagus into it laying the spears one by one crossways across the griddle The larger the spears the longer they'll take to cook. Large thicker spears will take around 5 minutes per side, small sprue asparagus around 2 minutes. For a range of sizes cook them together but remove the thinner spears earlier.

A lovely breakfast or light lunch

When blackened and still crunchy, not too soft, lift the asparagus onto a plate and sprinkle the pecorino over quickly, as evenly as possible. At least some of the cheese will melt. If you think you've under done the cheese grate more over. Drizzle a glug of olive oil over as evenly as possible and seal the plate quickly with cling film.

Now boil a pan of water and hard boil the eggs, leaving them for 8 minutes. Take them out and place them in cold water until they are cold (around 10 minutes).

Crack the shells by softly bashing and then rolling the eggs on the kitchen counter or chopping board and peeling and removing the shells and any membrane that remains on the eggs. Run them under a cold tap to remove any shell fragments, dry them with kitchen towel, and chop them very finely into small pieces.

Remove the cling film and lift half the spears onto a second plate using an egg slice. Sprinkle the chopped egg over each portion, followed by a little salt and you're good to go

A gorgeous dish, one of my favourites, that makes a great breakfast or light lunch. Delicious.

Broad bean fritters ▲

shelled broad bean pods, medium to large, fresh, 10 – 15, topped and tailed

gluten- free plain white flour, 100 gm

sweet paprika, 1 tbspn

black pepper, ground, lots, 25 twists of the pepper mill (or less if you prefer less hot)

salt, 1 tspn

oat milk, 160ml

vegetable oil, enough for depth in frying pan of ½cm

portions, 2 great snacks as a crisp or peanut alternative

NOTES: Broad bean pods do not keep well, going black soon after removing the beans. They don't last in the fridge, and they don't freeze well. So I think the best way of getting the most from your broad beans is to pod them the day before you need them – the beans do keep well in the fridge and freeze well – and make the fritters not longer than two or three hours later.

The quantities in the recipe may vary depending on how many pods you have, how big they are, and the size of your pan. So be prepared to add more to use all the pods.

As the flour takes up the oil quite readily during cooking, you'll need to make two batches (or use two pans is you want to eat both batches at the same time!)

Have a couple of pieces of kitchen towel to hand to wipe hands as you go. My sisters loved to help Mamá make these when they were small!

First slice the bean pods into 4cm pieces, on the diagonal.

Pour the flour onto a plate and sprinkle over the paprika, salt, and pepper, then mix together well using a spoon or plastic spatula.

Now pour the milk into a bowl, put the pan over a medium heat and add the oil.

Begin coating the bean pods by placing them on the flour and giving them a good mix round so they're well covered, then remove them to another plate individually, shaking them well to remove loose flour mix.

Make sure the bowl of milk is close to the plates of bean pods and flour mix.

When the oil is hot, take the flour- coated pods one at a time, dip them in the milk, then drag them through the flour so both sides are re-coated and place them in the pan, as quickly as you can.

After two or three minutes they'll be browning. Turn them individually using a fork or small thin tongues, and after another two or three minutes turn them again. After another minute or so they should be a really appetizing golden brown on both sides so lift them from the pan with a slotted spoon onto a plate with kitchen towel to dry them a little. If possible, better than crisps. Enjoy!

Broad bean meze ▲

broad beans, fresh, 10 - 12 pods podded

onions, 1 medium, finely chopped

garlic, 2 cloves, finely chopped

sage, 1 large sprig - 20 leaves, chopped

vegetable stock, as needed by the tbspn, up to ¼litre, for consistency

XV olive oil, 2 good glugs

salt & pepper to taste

portions, 6 or so snacks when spread onto crackers, 3 or so when used as a pasta sauce. Also wonderful as a dip with broad bean fritters (see previous recipe).

Put a frying pan over a medium heat and add the oil. When the oil is hot add the onions, garlic, and sage and fry until the onions are soft and translucent, around 5 minutes.

Add the broad beans and stir. Turn heat to low and fry for 15 minutes stirring occasionally. Use the back of a fork to lightly crush the beans then add 3 tablespoons of stock and simmer for 10 minutes, stirring occasionally.

Crush the mixture using the back of the fork again, add two more tablespoons of stock and stir in well, simmer for 5 minutes.

Spoon the mixture into a Pyrex bowl or jug and blend with a stick blender. You're looking for a consistency that will spread well on toast or crackers. If too dry, add a tablespoon of oil and blend again, if still too dry add 2 tablespoons of stock and give a final whizz.

Allow to cool before the first spreading. Enjoy!

Celeriac fritters ▲

celeriac, 1

good olive oil, 4 good slugs

salt, 2 teaspoons

4 portions, try 2 hot and leave 2 to have cold as a salad

Peel the celeriac, making sure you don't leave any skin or roots attached; but don't take off too much of the flesh. A potato peeler will take off much of the skin and a carefully applied sharp knife will take off the rooty bits.

Carefully slice the celeriac into 15mm slices, as evenly thick as possible across each slice. Because celeriac is so hard they are quite tough to cut through so be VERY careful the knife and celeriac don't slip while you are cutting as it will be quite easy to cut yourself if you are not. You will probably end up with 5 or 6 fritters. Scrunch salt over one side.

Heat two frying pans over medium heat and when hot add the olive oil. It should be around 5mm deep. When the oil is hot add 2 or 3 fritters to each pan, salted side down; they should start sizzling straight away.

Simply fry them for around 10 minutes, after which the cooked side of the fritters should be golden brown. Don't worry if they are beginning to blacken in places. Salt the top sides of the fritters then turn them and fry for around another 10 minutes until golden brown on the other side. Remove from pan and keep warm until ready to serve.

This is a surprisingly delicious way to serve celeriac; excellent as a base for pan fried lemon sole fillets, or cut into 15mm cubes and served cold as a salad.

Gnocchi

potatoes, medium, whole, unpeeled, 2 - 3, as near as you can get to 500 gm

egg, 1, lightly beaten

plain gluten-free flour, 100gm

+ flour for pressing and shaping

salt, 1 pinch

portions, 2

Preheat the oven to 200°C 180°C fan, when hot stab the potatoes with a fork on 4 sides, run them under the cold tap, and put them in the oven to bake for 1 hour.

Working with the potatoes, make the gnocchi dough while they're still hot. Start by slicing each of the potatoes in half and gently scooping out the potato and putting it into a bowl. I like to keep the skins intact and freeze them to use later . . . as . . . .well . . . potato skins! They're crispy, and great filled with a curry or bolognaise, heated up in the oven.

Add the salt, egg, and flour to the potato and mix well. Don't over-work the dough; stop mixing as soon as it comes together.

You can make the gnocchi on the kitchen counter. Just sprinkle the flour, then take the dough, place it on the flour and flatten it, shaping it as you flatten with the palms of your hands, into a square around 1.5cm, thick. Use a knife to cut the square into strips around 1.5cm wide so that you end up with square 'sausages'.

Flour your hands, the square sausages and the counter really well, then use the palms of your hands to roll each one into a cylinder. Now take a knife and cut each cylinder into pieces around 1.5 cm long.

Take a fork with a rounded end to its handle, lay the rounded end on top of one of your dough pieces so that around ½cm of dough is uncovered by the very end of your fork. Press the fork down, squashing out a U shape until there remains around ½cm of dough at the bottom. Well done, you've just made your first gnocchi!

Now continue until you've formed all the gnocchi and move them gently onto a plate. If you're not going to use them straight away cover them with cling film to stop them drying out. They also freeze well so you can put them into a freezer bag and straight into the freezer. Cook them straight from frozen.

Bring a large saucepan of salted water to the boil and slide the gnocchi gently in and stir round. Be careful not to overcrowd them or they'll stick together, they cook quickly so do it in 2 batches if you're in doubt. Best to give them space. They will cook quickly, just 1 – 3 minutes, and you 'll know when they're cooked when they float to the surface.

Take a plate and put a piece of kitchen towel onto it, and scoop out your gnocchi with a slotted spoon, laying them after a quick shake of the spoon to remove most of the moisture, onto the kitchen towel to absorb more water as it drains from them.

Mevagissey lighthouse at sunrise.

Hot and Herby Tomato Sauce ▲

My mother makes this recipe in great quantities when tomatoes are in plentiful supply in the greenhouses. It freezes well and brings a welcome taste of the sun on a cold winter's day.

ripe tomatoes, 20 cherry, 8 standard, chopped, stalks out

lemon, 1/2, juice of

green chilli, 1 small, finely chopped, no seeds

tarragon, 3 sprigs, chopped

chives, 1 small handful, chopped

chervil, 1 small handful, chopped

XV olive oil, 3 tbspns

salt and black pepper to taste

2 portions

Mix all the ingredients in a pan and simmer for 15 minutes. Whizz with a stick blender. Add boiling water by the teaspoonful to reach your preferred consistency.

Variation: you can substitute parsley for chervil but it doesn't work quite as well in this dish.

Use dill if you have it and can't get parsley or chervil. Chervil grows readily from seed and is an essential in a good herb omelette.

Magical field mushrooms ▲

small red chilli, 1, finely chopped

parsley, 1 handful, chopped

thyme, 5 sprigs, leaves chopped

large field mushrooms, 2, roughly chopped

garlic, 3 cloves finely chopped

double cream or oat cream, 3 tbsps

XV olive oil, 1 good glug

goats' butter, 1 small knob

2 large portions

This is amazingly tasty but really easy to cook, and so quick!

Heat the oil in a deep frying pan. Add the chilli, parsley and garlic and sweat for 5 minutes then add the butter. Add the cream and cook for 5 minutes.

Add the mushrooms, stir, cover (use foil folded down round the sides of the frying pan if you don't have a lid for it) and cook for 10 - 13 minutes.

Wonderful on toast.

Told you it was quick!!

Noodles

plain glute-free flour, 80gm, plus flour for rolling and sprinkling over

gram flour, 45 gm

water, 60gm

good olive oil, 1 tbspn

xanthan gum, ½ tbspn

salt, 1 good pinch

Portions, 2

Mix the dry ingredients in a large bowl. Add the water and use a metal pallet knife to mix into a dough. Add the oil and mix in well. Split the dough into 4, roll each piece into a ball by rolling between the palms of your hands.

Sprinkle flour generously over a cold rolling surface, place the first dough ball on the surface and press gently on it until around 2cm thick then shape it into a rectangle using the flat edges of your hands.

Roll the rectangle until it is noodle thin, frequently flouring the dough and the rolling pin. Now form into noodles by cutting into strips 1cm wide, and sprinkle them with flour. Repeat with the other 3 dough balls and you're ready to cook your noodles which will take just 2 – 3 minutes in boiling water.

The noodles are quite fragile, so place them gently into a large saucepan of boiling water, spread them about gently, return the water to a simmer and cook the noodles for 2 – 3 minutes. Lift your lovely noodles out of the pan gently, using an egg slice and slide them gently onto your plates.

Some of your noodles may well have broken because they are so fragile, but don't worry, they will all still be absolutely delicious.

Pak Choi, steamed with ginger ▲

pak choi, 2 bulbs

ginger, fresh, peeled, 10 thumbnail sized pieces, very finely sliced

salt, 2 pinches

Tamari soy sauce, 1 glug

portions, 2

This is another simple dish, great with plain cooked fish, and isn't overpoweringly spicy.

Try it with coriander mash and baked cod (bake fillets drizzled with good olive oil on a baking tray for 20-30 minutes, depending on thickness, at 170ºC, 150ºC fan). It is also good with fried or grilled pork chops.

First get the steamer water steaming, then chop each pak choi bulb into 4, lengthways, and lay in the steamer container. Place the ginger around and on top of the pak choi, then sprinkle with salt and drizzle the soy sauce over. Put the lid on the container, place over the steaming water and steam for 5 minutes.

Because this is so quick to cook, don't put the container over the steaming water until just before the main ingredient is ready.

Splenditious squash sauce ▲

butternut squash, 1/3, peeled, deseeded and small cubed, ½cm – 1cm

onions, 2 medium, finely chopped

garlic, 2 cloves, finely chopped

thyme, 1 large sprig

sage, 1 large sprig - 20 leaves, chopped

crème fraîche 2 dsps, or oat cream, 2dsps with 1 tsp lemon juice

mace, ground mace, ¼ tsp

vegetable stock, ¼litre

XV olive oil, 1 good glug

goats butter, 1knob

salt & pepper to taste

4 portions

Heat the oil in a deep frying pan. Add the garlic sweat for 5 minutes then add the squash, mace and herbs. Sweat for 10 minutes.

Add the stock and simmer for 25 minutes, stirring occasionally. Add the butter, salt and pepper and cook for further 10 minutes. Remove from the heat and stir in the crème fraîche or oat cream.

Wonderful with toast or crudites.

Slacken the mixture with a little pasta water for a great pasta sauce.

GLUTEN-FREE BAKING

Gluten-free soda bread, a staple star!

Crackers

These are perfect with cheese or broad bean or splenditious squash meze.

gram flour, 40gm

gluten-free self-raising flour, 190gm

table salt, 1 teaspoon

caster sugar, 1 teaspoon

xanthan gum, ¼

baking powder, 1 teaspoon

black pepper, 39 grinds of the mill

water, ½ cup, 125ml

extra virgin olive oil, 2 tablespoons

portions, this will make around 16 crackers approximately 30mm x 270mm long

Mix dry ingredients in a bowl with a balloon whisk. Add the oil and water and mix using a rubber spatula to form a dough.

Rest the dough for ½ hour. In the bowl on the side in the kitchen is fine.

Preheat oven to 220ºC 200°C fan.

Place a sheet of baking parchment the right size for your baking tray on the kitchen counter, sprinkle liberally with the flour, roll into a rough rectangle around 2mm thick. Use plenty of flour to keep dusting the rolling pin, as gluten-free dough is notorious for sticking!

Cut the rectangle into crackers the size and shape you are looking for, and LEAVE THEM ON THE PARCHMENT.

Gently slide the parchment onto a baking tray and place in the oven for around 15 minutes. Keep an eye on them. They may need a little longer until they have turned a light golden brown.

Remove from the oven and gently lift the crackers onto a cooling tray.

VARIATIONS

To vary the flavour of your crackers just mix in a tablespoon or two of any of the following with the dry ingredients before adding the oil and water:

Green coriander seeds, grated horseradish, fennel seeds, sesame seeds, finely chopped drained capers, finely chopped preserved lemon...

NOTE – depending on the size of your baking tray you may need to do the baking in two batches, or to use 2 trays if you have them.

ANOTHER NOTE: - if the crackers are slightly softer than you like them after cooking, or they should turn softer, go for a second baking, at the same temperature for just 4 minutes to crisp them up.

Gluten-free banana muffins

gluten-free plain flour, 150 gm

caster sugar, 75gm

salt, ¼ tspn

baking powder, 1 ½ tspn

flavourless oil: groundnut or rapeseed or sunflower, 60 ml

milk, goats' milk, soya or oat 120 ml

egg, 1 large, beaten

ripe banana, 1 large mashed

8 muffins

Preheat the oven to 220ºC, 200ºC fan

Mix all the dry ingredients in a large bowl with a balloon whisk. Mix the beaten egg, oil and milk in a jug or bowl and add to the dry, stir in but don't overdo it then stir in the banana.

Pour into muffin cases in the muffin tin - I use a Pyrex jug for this – to 2/3 full.

Bake for 5 minutes turn oven down to 180ºC, 160ºC fan for a further 15 minutes. Allow to cool slightly in tray then move onto a cold surface.

Variations: blueberries, raspberries, chopped mango in place of banana.

Gluten-free chocolate & vanilla syrup oat cookies

rolled oats, 165 gm

gluten-free plain flour, 60 gm

caster sugar, 75gm

soft dark brown sugar, 45 gm

salt, 1/4 tspn

baking powder, 1/2 tspn

cocoa powder, 2 tbspns

vanilla extract, 1 tspn

golden syrup, 1 tbspn

flavourless oil: groundnut or rapeseed or sunflower, 125ml

egg, 1 large, beaten

16-18 cookies

Preheat the oven to 190°C, 170°C fan

Mix all the dry ingredients in a large bowl with a balloon whisk.

Mix the beaten egg, oil, vanilla and syrup in jug or bowl and add to the dry ingredients, mixing well until you have a dark brown gloopy mass.

Spoon onto baking parchment lined baking trays using a dessertspoon. Bake for 15-20 minutes until just firm to the touch.

Remove from the oven and allow to cool on tray for 10 minutes before transferring them to a cooling rack.

Delicious, gluten-free . . . and fabulously chocolatey!

Crispy butter pastry

goats' butter, from freezer, 150gm

gluten-free plain flour, 200gm

xanthan gum, 2 large pinches

table salt, ½ teaspoon

water, cold, 10 - 12 tablespoons

portions. This makes sufficient pastry for 2 Cornish pasties (my recipe for these great pasties is on page 105), or around 10 Caden's Christmas sausage rolls (the recipe is on page 93).

Whisk the dry ingredients in a bowl. Coarse grate the butter, straight from frozen, sprinkling the grater with flour from time to time to maintain the edge. Mix using a cold metal palette knife, using an edge to slice through any lumps that might build up until the mixture has the appearance of rough bread crumbs.

Add 8 tablespoons of water and mix using the palette knife, then continue adding and mixing water one tablespoon at a time until the dough can be formed. It should not be too dry, nor should it runny.

Roll the dough into a ball and wrap in cling film, leave in fridge for 30 minutes. I always then give it five minutes then to warm slightly before rolling as it makes the rolling a little easier. Whatever you're making, roll out directly onto baking parchment and make sure you use lots of gluten-free plain flour on the parchment and rolling pin to avoid sticking.

Cooking time is around 45 - 50 minutes for pasties at 190°C, 170°C fan and 35 minutes for sausages rolls. Cook until they're a lovely light golden brown.

Pizza base, thin and crispy

gluten-free white bread flour, 190 gm

baking powder, 1½ teaspoons

table salt ½ teaspoon

caster sugar, 1½ teaspoons

xanthan gum, ¾ teaspoon

extra virgin olive oil, 1½ teaspoons

water, 150ml

portions - makes one 310mm diameter thin crust pizza base.

Preheat oven to 270ºC, 250°C fan. You need a very hot oven.

I make this on a pizza baking tray with holes in the base.

In a large bowl mix all the dry ingredients with a balloon whisk. Then add the oil and most of the water mixing into the dry. I use a small flexible rubber spatula for this. Add the last of the water gently mixing until the dough comes away from the sides of the bowl leaving them clean. If the dough is too wet just add a little more flour and mix. Place the dough in the fridge to chill for 30 minutes.

Remove dough from bowl onto floured baking parchment measured to just over the size of your pizza tray place on a board. You are going to flip the pizza onto the tray. Press the dough into a circle to fit your pizza baking tray using the side of a fist and your fingers to push. Place the pizza tray, inverted over the dough and flip the base onto the pizza tray. Peel off the baking parchment carefully keeping the paper close to the pizza. Bake in the hot oven for 5 minutes until the edges start to turn golden. Remove and set aside to cool before adding toppings.

Once you have loaded the base with the toppings of your choice, place back in the reheated oven for around 15 minutes.

PIZZA TOPPINGS

Just add your chosen topping to your cooled, part-baked pizza base and return to a very hot oven preheated to 270°C 250°C fan for 15 minutes.

Spicy beef & egg

raw beef, minced or finely chopped, 150gm fried with a small medium heat red chilli, ¼ finely chopped, no seeds until the meat has lost its redness, about 10 minutes. Season to taste.

chopped, tinned tomatoes, drained of juice, 150gm (keep the juice in the fridge for later use)

green pepper, ½ cut into strips, sweated in a little olive oil

large onion, 1, sliced in strips, sweated with the green pepper

button mushrooms, 6, sliced, tossed in Tamari soy sauce and left for 30 minutes.

capers, 3 teaspoons

black olives, 13, halved

buffalo mozzarella, 1, shredded

eggs, 2, with ½ the whites separated as in making mayonnaise

extra virgin olive oil, to drizzle

Spread the chopped tomato across the pizza base then add the onion and pepper, spicy meat, mushrooms, capers, olives and buffalo mozzarella. Drizzle with the oil.

Bake for 13 minutes, remove from the oven, pour the egg yolk and white onto the centre of the pizza, return to the oven for 2 minutes.

Remove from the oven and spread the egg across the pizza before slicing.

Spiced & herbed chicken

raw chicken, finely chopped, 150gm, fried with a small medium heat red chilli, ¼ finely chopped, no seeds, until the meat has lost its pinkness, about 10 minutes. Season to taste.

green coriander seeds, 2 teaspoons

basil, pinched out tops or finely chopped, 2 teaspoons

chopped, tinned tomatoes , 150gm, drained of juice (keep the juice in the fridge for later use)

green pepper, ½, cut into strips, sweated in a little olive oil

large onion, 1, sliced in strips, sweated with the green pepper

capers, 3 teaspoons

black olives, 13, halved

buffalo mozzarella, 1, shredded

extra virgin olive oil, to drizzle

Mix the spicy chicken with the green coriander seeds and basil. Spread the chopped tomato across the pizza base then add the onion and pepper, spicy chicken mix, capers, olives and mozzarella. Drizzle with the oil.

Bake for 15 minutes.

Fish & prawn with preserved lemon & mushy peas

One of my very favourite toppings is a bit off the wall! Instead of the traditional tomato base I use mushy peas. You will find the recipe, along with that for mushy peas, in my first book, The Little Cornish Fish & Seafood Cookbook.

Soda Bread

This loaf can be used for breadcrumbs wherever they are called for. Just use an end or cut a thick slice and finely chop. If you don't need them all, just freeze.

gluten-free white bread flour, 550 gm

baking powder, 3½ teaspoons

xanthan gum, 1 teaspoon

bicarbonate of soda, 1½ teaspoons

salt, 1½ teaspoons

lemon juice, 1½ tablespoons

clear runny honey, 2 teaspoons,

oat milk or sheeps' yoghurt or goats' yoghurt or milk, 550 ml

Note: if you don't have white bread flour use an equal amount of self-raising flour and add 1 additional teaspoon of xanthan gum.

portions, makes 1 loaf

Unlike most soda breads which are round, I prefer to make mine looking more like a conventional loaf, so I use a traditional 1kg loaf tin for the baking. Of course you can use the tin that suits you best.

Lately I have been using oat milk to great effect but any of the above liquid elements will work.

Pre heat the oven to 210°C, 190°C fan

Heat the yoghurt, milk or oat milk in a saucepan or the microwave until it is warm to the touch – 60 seconds full power in my microwave. Add the lemon juice and honey and stir well.

Whisk all the dry ingredients together in a mixing bowl with a balloon whisk. Switch to a rubber spatula and add the yoghurt/oat milk mix and stir to amalgamate. Sometimes I need to add a little goat's milk or plant-based milk to take up all the flour mix. You are looking for the consistency of mashed potato. No resting!

Tip and spoon the dough into the baking parchment lined tin - with custom-made loaf tin liners or dampened parchment to line - and smooth the top then stab the loaf with a hot knife or skewer all over right to the bottom. This lets the air out during cooking and helps to avoid splitting.

I find scalding the knife or skewer with boiling water helps it slide out without dragging the dough with it.

Bake for 31 minutes. Take the bread from the oven, remove it from the tin and put it onto a cooling tray.

There may well be a split in the loaf, don't worry, this is normal!

The chimneys at Geevor, not for bread ovens, but tin!

And Finally

Crab and 3 way cucumber soup

I first made this when Mamá brought in a large cucumber from the greenhouse as my sister Eva arrived home with the Friday shellfish and fish from St Ives. There was also a portion of crab sauce leftover from a pasta supper sitting in the fridge. It was a great success with everyone, but especially with Eva, who absolutely loves it, especially the fried cucumber!!

shellfish stock, 1 litre

cucumber, 1 large, prepared as below

onion, 1 medium, chopped

potatoes, 2 medium, small diced

white crabmeat, 2 handfuls

brown crabmeat, 1 handful

crab sauce, 2 cups (see page 78). If you make a bigger batch, freeze the rest

lemon, 1/4 juice of, 1/4 zest of

sumac, 1 tspn

goats' butter, 1 knob

flavourless oil, 1 glug

salt & white pepper to taste

4 portions

Prepare the cucumber. Top and tail the cucumber then peel and thinly slice 5cm and set the slices aside. Slice the remaining cucumber into 2 halves lengthways and deseed the two halves using a teaspoon to scoop out the seeds into teaspoon sized pieces as far as possible. Set the seeds aside.

Chop the cucumber halves into pieces around 2 - 3 cm long, then cut the pieces into logs 2 - 3 cm by ½ cm. Fry half the logs in butter until lightly golden and set aside.

In a large pan, fry the onion and 1/3 of the potato in butter and oil until soft (10 - 15 minutes). Add the stock, simmer for 5 minutes then whizz with a stick blender until smooth.

Add the lemon zest, crab sauce, sumac, cucumber seeds, remaining potato, brown crabmeat and simmer for 5 minutes. Now add the uncooked cucumber logs and simmer for a further 5 minutes. Add the lemon juice, white crabmeat, and the fried cucumber logs. Season

Serve, garnished with the cucumber slices.

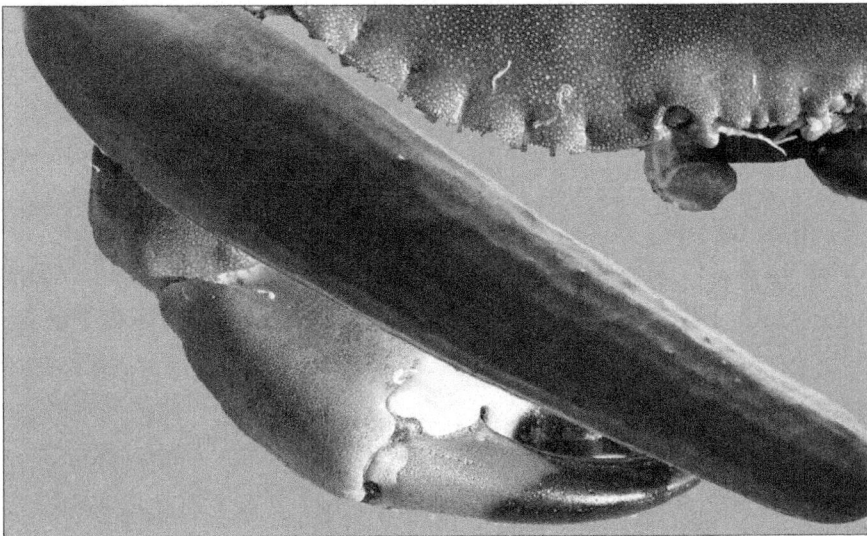

Crab and the ever-flexible cucumber – a great combination

I hope you enjoy the crab and 3 way cucumber soup as much as Eva does, and if it is your first time frying cucumber I wonder if it is as much of a pleasant surprise as it always is to us!

More about Beatriz Treloar and the DI Treloar Cornish crime thriller series

About Beatriz Treloar

Beatriz Treloar is the exciting young head chef at SEAFOOD ON STILTS and THE CUTTLEFISH CAFE in St Ives, Cornwall. She first appears in the second DI Treloar crime thriller, the award-winning BROKEN DOVE.

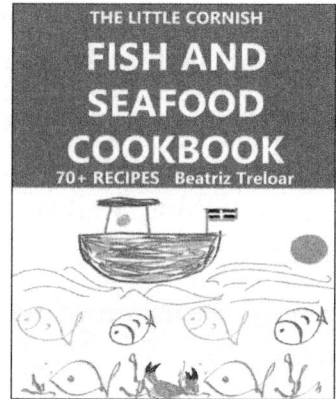

Situated on the quayside in St Ives, the restaurant sits above the café's terrace – hence the stilts. Beatriz is the youngest of DI Félipe Treloar's three sisters.

Beatriz's first book was The Little Cornish Fish and Seafood Cookbook, it's available at Amazon in paperback, hardback and kindle editions.

About the DI Treloar Cornish Crime Thrillers

The DI Treloar series written by L A Kent follows the exploits of the detective as he and his team face serious, challenging crimes in Cornwall. There are four books to date with a fifth, FALLEN KESTREL, the Marazion Murders, to be published in 2024:

Rogue Flamingo – The Mevagissey murders

Broken Dove – The St Ives murders

Silent Gull – The Fowey murders

Sad Pelican – The Padstow murders

To get your Cornish murder mystery reading juices flowing the book covers are on the next page. They are available as paperbacks and for Kindle and can be bought from Amazon.

The Cornish setting book covers are shown overleaf and you can read more about LA Kent and the strong-minded and some would say maverick DI Treloar at www.lakent.co.uk.

Here are the DI Treloar series book covers to whet your appetite, just go to Amazon to get your copies.

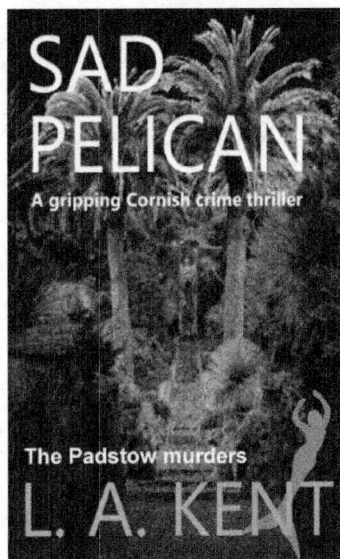

ROGUE FLAMINGO
A gripping Cornish crime thriller
The Mevagissey murders
L. A. KENT

BROKEN DOVE
A disturbing Cornish crime thriller
The St. Ives murders
L. A. KENT

SILENT GULL
A chilling Cornish crime thriller
The Fowey murders
L. A. KENT

SAD PELICAN
A gripping Cornish crime thriller
The Padstow murders
L. A. KENT

Copyright

The authors also publish under the pseudonym L. A. Kent, writing crime thrillers – the DI Treloar Cornish crime thriller series. Beatriz Treloar is DI Treloar's sister. You can read more about the series and subscribe to the L. A. Kent news updates on the web site www.lakent.co.uk. You will receive a free dossier written by HM Secret Services on DI Treloar when you subscribe to the newsletter.

Index

Printed in Great Britain
by Amazon